ane act of admission herevpon that we may enjoy ye priviledges & immunities
of ye Society

Hugh Blair   Ja: Reid

Robert Watwood   David Noish

Alexander Sauvie   William Cock   Georg Balfour

George Clark   Georg Bell   Hugh Blackie

John I Clerk

An: Tennant   Alexr Campbell   John Caitt

Ro:ssord +

Robert Broune   Jo: Nasmyth

Thomas Ashcroft   Thomas Kor   David Lestern

John Lindsay   John Grindus   James Fergus

Jo: Follie   James Clerk   Ja: Gib

Ha: Elphinston +

James Gowdon   Jno Drummond   James Aitkine

L Cunninghame   1682:   James Caitt   Alexander Chancelor

Jo: Hunter   Laurence Donaldson   A H:ALLAN

Blair   Jo: Broune   John armstrong

Falconar   John Hill +   Tho young

James Roth   George Hunterlowne

John Corbet

Robert Baird   Gibson

Hugh Campbell   John henderson

G. Drummond   William Horsale

Arch: Walker   Arbuthnot   Entered 83

Ja: on:

THE
EDINBURGH
MERCHANT
COMPANY

Rosemary — with best wishes
from Rosalind.

See pages ix and 124.

THE
EDINBURGH
MERCHANT
COMPANY

A STORY OF ENDEAVOUR
AND ACHIEVEMENT

Rosalind K. Marshall

FRONTISPIECE.
Silver gilt nef (ship centrepiece) presented by
Master Gilbert Archer, 1933 (The Merchant Company;
John McKenzie Photography)

First published in Great Britain in 2015 by
John Donald, an imprint of Birlinn Ltd

West Newington House
10 Newington Road
Edinburgh
EH9 1QS

www.birlinn.co.uk

ISBN: 978 1 906566 96 8

British Library Cataloguing-in-Publication Data
A catalogue record for this book is available
on request from the British Library

Typeset by Mark Blackadder

Printed and bound by Livonia Print, Latvia

Contents

·A.D.· ·1681·

·TERRAQUE· ·MARIQUE·

Foreword

Although The Company of Merchants of the City of Edinburgh can trace its roots back to the late thirteenth century, its history really began with the granting of its Royal Charter by King Charles ll in 1681. Since that time it has had a wonderful history rich in philanthropy, adventure, enterprise and bold decisions being taken by its distinguished list of members, many of whom went on to achieve fame and fortune and leave their mark on the city, Scotland and indeed the whole of the UK.

Much of the history is documented in detailed minutes of every meeting, meticulously recorded and bound into scores of leather-clad volumes beginning with the copperplate, hand-written minutes of the very first meeting on 1 December 1681. But much is also anecdotal, full of stories, tales and yarns which add to the colour, traditions and pageantry behind one of Edinburgh's oldest institutions.

Although minutes will continue to record the formal business of the Company, it is absolutely vital that these stories and anecdotes are not lost to future generations. The history of The Merchant Company from 1681 to 1902 is well documented in a book by Alexander Heron, but as Master I felt it was time to continue with the story of the last hundred years or so before it gets lost in the annals of time. Heron's history effectively ends with the death of Master John Macmillan at a Company dinner on 8 January 1901, and this new book begins with the same event, ensuring seamless continuity in the fascinating story of this ancient and venerable organisation.

For this project we were very fortunate to secure the services of the well-known author and historian Dr Rosalind K Marshall, whose painstaking research into Merchant Company history and ability to turn historical fact into an easily read story has produced this excellent account of The Company of Merchants of the City of Edinburgh.

Ian M.L. Watson
Master, 2013–2015

Author's Acknowledgements

I have pleasure in thanking all those who helped in the making of this book. Master Ian Watson himself assembled all the illustrations, and various office-bearers past and present spoke to me or sent me information about the history of The Merchant Company, particularly Old Master Brian Adair, Old Master Gilbert Baird Archer and Secretary and Chamberlain Gregor Murray. Old Masters Ian Adam, Sir Ewan Brown, Ian Darling and Douglas Kinloch Anderson told me about their time with the Company. Likewise I was given valuable information by former Secretaries and Chamberlains Alistair Beattie and Robin Wilson; former Assistant Secretary Maurice Berrill; the Secretary and Chamberlain's PA Kathleen Callachan and the former Hall Keeper, the late Glynn Kay.

I thank the Very Reverend Gilleasbuig Macmillan KCVO for his knowledgeable comments and I had helpful conversations with Dr Elizabeth Cumming and Rosemary Colquhoun WS (Mrs Woodroffe). Dr Frances Shaw, with characteristic efficiency, arranged access to documents in the Company Archives lodged with Edinburgh City Archives, and Old Master Douglas Kinloch Anderson and Alan Macmillan kindly allowed me to look at relevant correspondence, invitations and scrapbooks in their family papers. Assistant Deirdre Kinloch Anderson gave me a copy of her handsome book about the history of the family firm, and I was able to read recollections previously sent in to the Company by Margaret Allan, Dawn Burrows, Robin Salvesen, Sir James Stirling, Patrick Tobin and Robin Wilson, as well as a short paper produced in 2013 by 11 of the Mary Erskine girls under the supervision of Sarah Horrix, their Biology Teacher and Form Tutor, as a result of their project on the potential closure of their school in 1975.

OPPOSITE.
Merchants' Hall Vault
(The Merchant Company;
© John McKenzie
Photography)

R.K.M.

CHAPTER 1

Across the Centuries: 1260–1900

On 8 January 1901, members of The Merchant Company of Edinburgh were happily preparing for their Annual Dinner in their Hanover Street Hall. This was always a pleasurable occasion, and there had been a particular excitement attached to the New Year celebrations the previous week, for 1 January saw the start of a new century. While white linen cloths were laid on the long tables in the elegant, domed hall, ready to be set out with the Company's silver gilt plate, the Master was busy attending a meeting about the important subject of Commercial Education. That evening he would, of course, preside at the dinner. It would be a large gathering, and the principal guest would be Alexander, 6th Lord Balfour of Burleigh, the distinguished politician who was Secretary of State for Scotland.

Master John Macmillan was himself a very well-known figure in Scottish business circles. Now 57 years old, he had been born in Dalkeith in 1843, the son of a successful cattle dealer. When he was in his teens, he was apprenticed to the famous firm of Andrew Melrose and Company, tea importers. He discovered that he had a natural aptitude for tea blending and when he was still only in his early twenties he was given sole responsibility for Melrose's entire buying and blending activities. Soon, he was recognised as Scotland's leading authority on Indian teas. As befitted someone of his standing, he lived in Corstorphine Hill House, better known to us today as the handsome Mansion House in the grounds of what is now Edinburgh Zoo. There, he and his wife, Jessie Chrystal Finlayson, an Edinburgh minister's daughter, brought up their typically large Victorian family of eight sons and one daughter. Their household was completed by a nurse, a housemaid, a cook, a table maid and a laundry maid, with their coachman living in the gatehouse. The motor car was a very new invention and prosperous families still relied upon their own coaches. It would not be until the end of 1903 that Lord Justice-Clerk Macdonald's private car would be the first in Edinburgh to gain a registered number plate. As for public transport, there were horse-drawn trams, and in recent months cable trams had been introduced, with many complaints about their liability to break down at any moment.

Jessie Macmillan died in 1894, and three years later her husband married again. His second wife, a few years younger than himself, was a German lady, Alwine Anna Franziska Amtsberg, who had recently been

OPPOSITE TOP.
The Merchants' Hall, Hanover Street
(© Steven Parry Donald Photography)

OPPOSITE BOTTOM.
Corstorphine Hill House, now The
Mansion House at Edinburgh Zoo
(© RCAHMS Licensor
www.rcahms.gov.uk)

ABOVE.
Master John Macmillan's nine
children (Courtesy of the Macmillan
Family Collection)

employed as a governess at Malleny House, Currie. Macmillan's public career continued to flourish, and it was in 1899 that he became Master of The Merchant Company, combining his demanding new role with his business duties. He attended the Merchants' Hall almost every day, chairing more than two hundred Company meetings each year as well as leading important business deputations, representing the Company on private occasions and attending social functions. He had always been deeply interested in education, perhaps not surprisingly in view of his own nine children, and now he became involved with one of the leading issues of the day.

Businessmen were concerned that boys entering the world of commerce had been taught Latin and Greek as their principal subjects – and what use were these in business affairs? Schools should be paying proper attention to modern languages, so that businessmen could speak to customers in their own tongue. They should be familiar with the geography of the world, and future clerks should learn book-keeping and shorthand skills. Master Macmillan enthusiastically chaired a joint sub-committee on Commercial Education, consisting of representatives

Corstorphine Parish Church
(© Rebecca Scott of Steven
Parry Donald Photography)

fering from heart trouble, and the previous autumn he had been forced to take a long rest. However, he had told a friend that he was looking forward to the Annual Dinner, and in the evening he joined the others in the Hall for the kind of lavish banquet fashionable at that time, each course accompanied by an appropriate wine. The meal began with oysters, turtle soup and then turbot in lobster sauce. Glasses of Chablis were drunk with the oysters, there was sherry with the turtle soup and hock with the turbot. Champagne followed, with Timbales à la Rothschild (sweetbreads), Suprême of pheasant, Saddle of mutton, and Ortolans – a French delicacy consisting of little songbirds. Charlotte Russe, liqueur jellies and sherry appeared next, then Croustades à l'Indienne were set before the diners, along with port. More sherry arrived with the cheeses, liqueurs were available with the ices, and claret came with dessert. Lord Salvesen, a leading Scottish judge, would later recall that not everyone could manage to eat their way through the entire menu on such occasions, so some people would miss out one or two of the courses. During the meal, Mr Henry Dambmann's small string ensemble provided live music ranging from a Spanish march to a selection entitled 'Merrie England', with a vocalist named Robert Burnett singing a series of Scottish songs.

Finally tea and coffee were served, and Master Macmillan stood up to give the first toast of the evening, to the Queen. Victoria was nearing the end of her long and prosperous reign now, but the Company's sense of loyalty to her was palpable. His speech successfully delivered, the Master sank back into his chair and, to the horror of the assembled members, closed his eyes, murmured, 'I am gone,' and lost consciousness. Several doctors who were present rushed forward to try to revive him, but without success. As his death

of The Merchant Company itself, along with others from Edinburgh and Leith Chambers of Commerce, and it was he who signed their published report in 1900, regretting the lack of appropriate training.

After his lengthy meeting about Commercial Education on the morning of 8 January, Master Macmillan was probably feeling exhausted. For several years he had been suf-

certificate records, he had died of a sudden stroke. Amidst the general confusion, Lord Balfour of Burleigh took charge and told everyone to go home. There was nothing more they could do.

The funeral took place four days later, with the *Scotsman* newspaper reporting that it was 'one of the most imposing seen in recent years'. More than 700 mourners assembled at the late Master's house. There were about 60 private coaches, and 350 pupils of The Merchant Company boys' schools lined the drive. After two short services indoors, John Macmillan's eight sons carried their father's polished oak coffin out to the hearse, which was drawn by two horses. At 2.30 on that winter afternoon they set out for the nearby Corstorphine Parish Church, watched by a large crowd. The cortège, almost a mile long, was led by a dozen boys in Highland dress, from the nearby Murrayfield Home of the Royal Society for the Prevention of Cruelty to Children.

The representatives of many public organisations also took part. The office-bearers of The Merchant Company were, of course, prominently placed. Sir James Steel, Lord Provost of Edinburgh, the magistrates and town council were all there, breaking their customary rule of attending formally only the funerals of their own members. Richard Mackie, Provost of Leith, was present, wearing his robes, and there were representatives of the Senate of Edinburgh University, both Edinburgh and Leith Chambers of Commerce, the Edinburgh Agricultural Association and the teaching staff of The Merchant Company Schools. In his eulogy, the minister paid tribute to Master Macmillan's calm, quiet dignity and his high ideals. He was buried in the churchyard and, the following day, the minister of Palmerston Place Church spoke of how he had been 'cut down in the full maturity of his manhood',

praising his friendly and genial personality and his kindness to widows and the fatherless.

The family erected a large Celtic cross over the grave, commemorating both Master Macmillan and his first wife, and in 1905 two stained-glass windows in their honour were inserted in the church itself. The Merchant Company, for their part, commissioned their

Memorial to Master John Macmillan in Corstorphine Churchyard (© Rebecca Scott of Steven Parry Donald Photography)

own memorial, in the form of a fine bust which sits in the hall of the Hanover Street building. It was placed there in 1903, on its own specially designed plinth. The members of The Merchant Company had voluntarily subscribed to the cost, which was £105 (just over £6,000 in present-day terms). The sculptor was the well-known David Watson Stevenson, who had helped Sir John Steell to create the Prince Albert Memorial in Charlotte Square Gardens and was best known for his statue of William Wallace at the Wallace Monument, Stirling.

Master Macmillan's memory would be kept alive in other ways too: three of his sons joined Melrose & Company, two of them becoming members of The Merchant Company, while his grandson, William Grierson Macmillan, would become Master in 1968. His only daughter, Chrystal, found fame in a different way. She was the first female mathematics and science graduate of Edinburgh University, studied in Berlin, took another degree at Edinburgh (in philosophy) and was a keen supporter of the Votes for Women movement. Founder of the Women's International League for Peace and Freedom, she subsequently became one of the first women barristers of the Inner Temple in London. In 2008, when Edinburgh University refurbished one of the old Medical School buildings on the north side of George Square to house the School of Social and Political Science, they named it in her honour.

Describing her father's funeral, the *Scotsman* had observed that its impressive nature could be attributed not only to his sudden, tragic death but to his position as Master of The Merchant Company. So how had the Company come to occupy such a prominent place in Edinburgh business life and, indeed, how had it all begun?

The Merchant Company has a long and prestigious history, dating back over 800 years, for although its royal charter was not granted until 1681, its origins lay in the late thirteenth century. At that time, the only people in Scotland allowed to take part in the country's foreign trade were the merchant burgesses of the royal burghs, those small towns which enjoyed royal protection and had been granted special privileges by the king. In return, the merchants were heavily taxed, and so they were making an important contribution to the Crown's revenues. Edinburgh, although not yet Scotland's fixed capital, was one such royal burgh and its leading merchants exported wool and hides, their vessels returning to the town's port of Leith with Scandinavian timber for building purposes, fine French wines, elegant ready-made clothing from Flanders and exotic spices which had initially been imported from the Orient to places like Antwerp and London. Not every merchant burgess was rich enough to engage in foreign trade, of course, but those who did could make a fortune.

Anxious to protect their monopoly, fend off illegal competition and give each other mutual support, the Edinburgh merchants banded together in about 1260 to form a Merchant Guild. As part of their obligations they made provision for their colleagues' widows and fatherless children, and they had a close connection with Edinburgh's parish church of St Giles'. The plague, violence and the primitive state of medical knowledge meant that life expectancy was very low at that time, with all too many people dying in their thirties. Scotland was a Catholic country and the Merchant Guild maintained their own altar in St Giles', where they could attend Masses and pray for themselves and their dead relatives and friends. The Guild members were responsible for paying their chaplain. If any of them broke their own regulations they were fined, and the fines went towards the upkeep of the church. When they died, they

OPPOSITE.
Bust of John Macmillan by David Watson Stevenson, 1903 (The Merchant Company; © John McKenzie Photography)

to have sent twin babies to the Island of Inchkeith with a nurse who was deaf and dumb, to see what language they would use when they began to speak. Would it be Latin, perhaps, or even Hebrew, rather than Scots? Whatever the truth of this anecdote, it does give us a hint of James's famously wide-ranging intellectual curiosity.

Monarchs lived a peripatetic existence in those days, moving from one royal castle or palace to the next, but Edinburgh became the fixed capital during James IV's reign and he and his Court were often to be found in the Castle or at Holyroodhouse, with the result that the merchants were personally known to the Royal Household, their leading customer. A business ledger kept by one of them, Andrew Halyburton, from 1492 until 1503, exists to this day and shows that he was sending back from Flanders (where he had settled) a wide range of luxury items including clothing, wine, pepper, ginger, feather mattresses and cushions. He even imported ecclesiastical vestments and elaborate tombstones. His ledger does not record his customers' names, but there can be little doubt that at least some of his cargoes were intended for King James IV.

That remains speculation, of course, but we do have one tiny piece of definite evidence which proves that the members of the Merchant Guild were well known to the King himself. This takes the form of a brief entry in the Lord High Treasurer's Accounts, which recorded the monarch's expenditure. It says that in 1501, £7 was spent on two ells of crimson satin to make the King's hood, when he became 'a brother to the Holy Blood'. Some years earlier, a number of members had formed the Confraternity of the Holy Blood – a confraternity being a group of devout lay people connected with a church, who came together for charitable and religious purposes. Wearing hooded crimson robes, the

were buried as close to their altar as possible, and special commemorative Masses were sung there each year for the welfare of their souls.

In all their activities, the Merchant Guild had a close link with royalty. James IV, for instance, who ruled Scotland from 1488 until 1513, was no distant, unapproachable figure. That affable, energetic and effective monarch spoke eight languages (including Gaelic) and took a keen interest in everything from dentistry and artillery to surgery and alchemy, paying some of his subjects to allow him to pull out troublesome teeth. He is even said

Confraternity of the Holy Blood could attend a special Mass each Wednesday in St Giles' at their altar. Of course King James would not have been there every week, any more than the busy merchants would have been; but he often sent alms, and for him to have become a brother of the Confraternity indicates that he was anxious to give them his patronage.

In 1513 James IV was tragically killed at the Battle of Flodden, but the Merchant Guild was going from strength to strength. Its Confraternity had flourished to such an extent that they needed more space, and moved to the newly built Holy Blood Aisle on the south side of St Giles', which had probably been constructed at their expense. We know that their altar there was richly furnished with a silver gilt chalice, a silver cross and other special ornaments, no doubt imported from the continent by the Guild. The famous Fetternear Banner depicting the crucified Christ, now in the National Museums of Scotland, belonged there too. With the Reformation of 1560, all the altars were taken away, but part of the Holy Blood Aisle still exists and bears a wooden plaque with its name. Despite the change in circumstances since the Reformation, the present-day Church of Scotland service of the Kirking of the Master of The Merchant Company is, in its own way, an echo of the connection between the medieval Merchant Guild and St Giles'.

By the 1530s, the Edinburgh merchants were in control of 80% of Scotland's foreign trade, Leith had become the country's main gateway to Europe and wealth had brought the Merchant Guild municipal influence as well as royal patronage. Almost all the members of the town council came from this elite group of businessmen, and naturally they elected their own colleagues as the Provost, Bailies and Dean of Guild. That was very much resented in some quarters, particularly by the local craftsmen. They had always objected loudly to the limitations imposed on their own activities by the Guild's trading monopoly and, grouping together as individual Incorporated Trades, the goldsmiths, the masons, the tailors, the candlemakers and others challenged the merchants' dominance of the town council while, for their part, the merchants condemned the craftsmen's defiance. At the Reformation in 1560, benches were installed in St Giles' so that the congregation could sit while they listened to John Knox's hour-long sermons. The town council organised the new seating arrangements, saying that 'honest merchants and honest craftsmen' were to 'place and set themselves together, as loving brethren and friends'.

That proved to be a pious hope rather than a realistic expectation. The rivalry between the two groups was as vehement as ever, and matters came to a head in 1582 when there was an alarming riot at the time of the burgh election, leading to the intervention of the King himself. James VI was only 16 years old, and he came from a distinctly dysfunctional background. His mother, Mary, Queen of Scots, had been forced to abdicate and flee the country after she was suspected of murdering his father, Lord Darnley. However, James was a shrewd and highly intelligent youth who would grow up to be Scotland's most astute monarch. He decided that the craftsmen must be given greater liberties. Certainly the Provost of Edinburgh, four Bailies, the Dean of Guild and the Treasurer of the town council would continue to be chosen from among the merchants, but of the 18 town councillors, eight would in future be craftsmen and both groups would be represented in Parliament. His decision was ratified the following year in an official document known as a Decreet Arbitral.

When James inherited the throne of England in 1603 and went south, many things changed. Scotland's Parliament and Privy

OPPOSITE.
King James VI of Scotland and I of England by an unknown artist (Scottish National Portrait Gallery)

Council still met in Edinburgh, but the Court had moved to London, which meant that the nobility would usually spend the winter months there, seeking audiences to beg the monarch for additional titles, property and other sources of income. They also took the opportunity of shopping for the wide range of luxury goods available there, shipping home new furniture for their castles, plants for their gardens, clothes for their wives and toys for their children. The Edinburgh merchants suffered as a result, but worse was to follow.

After James died in 1625, his throne was inherited by his son, Charles I, who lacked his father's political acumen. Civil war resulted, Charles was deposed and executed, and Oliver Cromwell ruled both Scotland and England as Lord Protector. Even the most

prosperous Edinburgh merchants found it difficult to retain their resources in these disturbed trading conditions. Sir William Dick of Braid was the richest merchant in the whole of Scotland, thanks to his exceptional entrepreneurial skills and his money-lending activities. He rented a very large and extremely expensive house in Kintore Close, and he owned the pink-washed sixteenth-century house which is now part of the complex at Craighouse in Morningside. During his long career he served as a Bailie, Treasurer and twice as Provost of Edinburgh – but he would die a bankrupt in 1655, the result of lending huge sums of money to the Covenanters, who opposed royal ecclesiastical policies.

The restoration of the monarchy in 1660 brought a greater stability, but the post-war world was different now, and it was increas-

ingly felt that the privileges enjoyed by the royal burghs were no longer appropriate. In 1672 an Act of Parliament was passed declaring that, in future, anyone could engage in foreign trade. The only imported items specifically reserved to the Edinburgh merchant burgesses were silks, wines, wax, spices and dyestuffs. The power of the royal burghs was obviously waning and, against that background, both James VI and Charles I had tried to encourage the Edinburgh merchants to form a company and apply for a royal charter. Confident of their position, they had not thought it necessary, but in 1681 some of them decided to act, possibly because the Merchant Guild had lost its rights and powers of self-government in the sixteenth century, when the town council took over the appointment of its office-bearers. At any rate,

the merchants involved in the cloth trade now petitioned the restored King Charles II for the necessary charter which would make them into an official Company. This was granted on 19 October 1681, and The Merchant Company of Edinburgh was founded.

On 1 December the new Company met for the first time. A picture of the occasion, as imagined by the nineteenth-century artist William Hole, who painted the Scottish historical murals in Edinburgh City Chambers and in the Scottish National Portrait Gallery, now hangs in the Court Room of the Merchants' Hall. The man in red standing behind the table with a chain of office round his neck is Sir James Fleming, for he was the Lord Provost and presided at the meeting. The figure in the foreground in a black gown represents Hugh Stevenson, who was Clerk

TOP.
The Court Room in the Merchants' Hall, with William Hole painting above fireplace (© Steven Parry Donald Photography)

ABOVE.
The Merchant Company Coat of Arms above the William Hole painting in the Court Room (© Steven Parry Donald Photography)

Assistants and a Treasurer were also chosen.

All those applying to be members had to be burgesses and guild brothers involved in trading in cloth or other merchandise connected with clothing. Members would be admitted on payment of £12 Scots entry money, with a further £6 Scots due four times a year. (At that time, one pound Scots was worth a twelfth of a pound sterling.) Along with voluntary contributions and fines imposed for drunkenness, swearing or absence from meetings, these funds would be disbursed for the good of the Company and as assistance to 'decayed members', their impoverished widows and children. With the emphasis on monopoly and on charity to members, these stipulations were very much a continuation of the rules of the medieval Merchant Guild and would in future become an increasing preoccupation.

In 1693, the Company received its coat of arms from the Lord Lyon. Very familiar to members today, its pair of sea unicorns supported a shield featuring, amongst other symbols, a sailing ship and an arm emerging from a cloud holding a pair of scales, with the pans flanking two of the ell rods used for measuring cloth. At the very top was a globe, symbolising world trade and the Latin motto 'Terra marique', meaning 'By land and sea'. Nowadays the Latin words have been changed to 'Terraque marique', without altering the meaning at all. The significance of the emblem of the Company, the Stock of Broom, is less clear. Various explanations have been offered, the most plausible being that broom is a modest shrub but with a great tendency to increase.

It is interesting to note that in the decade after the granting of the charter, several women as well as men became members. It was not at all unusual to find women in business in the seventeenth century. They were very often widows who had taken on their

Depute of the Scottish Privy Council. He not only read out the vital charter, but was elected Clerk of the Company. The somewhat sedate-looking witnesses to the scene actually consisted of no fewer than 82 merchants who had crowded into the High Council House, part of the Court of Session, along with the first Bailie and the Lord Dean of Guild. They all signed the Roll Book and a member named George Drummond, who would become Provost of Edinburgh two years later, was elected first Master of the Company. Twelve

husbands' shop-keeping businesses, and presumably those found on the Merchant Company Roll were selling cloth, clothing or accessories. Eleanor Martin, the widow of John Duncan, was the first to sign, just two months after the royal charter was granted. Elizabeth Bennet, shopkeeper, also became a member, as did Jean Jardine, who had remarried but was apparently still carrying on her business. Three other women paid their entry fees, 'having the Dean of Guild's licence', whatever that involved; and although some of the male members could not sign their names and had to make their marks instead, the women mentioned were all literate and well able to add their signatures. The last woman to feature was Mary Campbell, who by 1701 had married Robert Lightbody. She had paid her fees to the Company, but she now assigned them to him, allowing him to benefit from membership, and so he took over from her and signed the Roll. After that, there would be no more women members until the twentieth century.

In keeping with the terms of the royal charter, the Company now began to look for its own premises. At first they continued to meet in the High Council House, but membership was nearing three hundred and a more spacious property was required. In the seventeenth century the most fashionable street in Edinburgh was the Cowgate, where a number of the aristocracy had their houses. There was no George IV Bridge in those days to overshadow the street below; instead, where the south pier of the Bridge now stands, there was a very substantial fifteenth-century building which later belonged to one of James VI's leading courtiers. Thomas, 1st Earl of Haddington had been President of the Court of Session. His house had a great hall, which would be ideal for meetings of the entire Company and other rooms which could be used for storage, the surplus

chambers being let out to suitable tenants. Outside was an unkempt piece of ground.

The house was now the property of Andrew Crawford, Sheriff Clerk of Linlithgow. Robert Blackwood, a prominent merchant, purchased it on behalf of the Company in 1691. The ceiling of the great hall was in need of repair, so it was re-plastered, and the well-known Bailie Alexander Brand provided expensive Spanish leather hangings for its walls. The ground outside was transformed into an attractive, tree-lined bowling green, and the Countess of Lauderdale was one of the first tenants of the vacant sets of rooms. In fact, the entire Company assembled together only two or three times a year, and when the office-bearers met every Tuesday,

The first Merchant Company Hall, in the Cowgate of Edinburgh (The Merchant Company Archive)

at eight o'clock in the morning, it was usually in one of the fashionable new coffee houses in the vicinity of Parliament Square.

By now, donations for charitable purposes were beginning to flow in. These came not only from members but from local people and even from business contacts in London who were impressed by The Merchant Company's status and its reputation for integrity. Some of the gifts took the form of legacies. In 1693, for example, David Aikenhead, a Scottish merchant in Poland, left £3,500 Scots, primarily to help impoverished merchants over the age of 50. Other gifts came from the living, and the Company had, of course, a responsibility towards the young as well as to the old. They had not been involved in the establishment of a home for fatherless boys, George Heriot's Hospital, which was funded with money left by the celebrated royal jeweller of that name. The word 'hospital' had no medical connotations in this context, but was an alms-house where the children would be cared for and taught. However, the Company's thoughts began to turn to the idea of a similar home for girls when in 1694 Mary Erskine, an Edinburgh businesswoman, offered them 10,000 merks 'for the maintenance of burgess children of the female sex'. (A Scottish merk was worth 13 shillings and 4 pence Scots.)

Four years after the death of her first husband James Kennedy, a solicitor, in 1671, Mary Erskine had married James Hair, an apothecary, but he died in 1683. In order to support herself and her young daughter Euphemia, she took over his business and in addition made a fortune by moneylending. Philanthropic by nature, she resolved to set up a home for the 7- to 14-year-old daughters of deceased or impoverished merchant burgesses of Edinburgh. She could not do all this by herself, and so she approached The Merchant Company. Impressed with her initiative, they held discussions with her. They estimated that it would cost about £20,000 Scots to put the plans into practice and they advertised successfully for additional donations. Those who gave the most generous sums would be allowed to nominate candidates for vacancies in the hospital.

By 1695 everything was ready and the Merchant Maiden Hospital was founded, with the girls lodging in the gallery above the Great Hall in the Company's Cowgate building, and in one of the cellars which had a kitchen chimney in it. This accommodation soon proved inadequate, and in 1706 Mary Erskine came to the rescue and purchased for the Hospital a substantial house with a garden, just outside the town wall in the Bristo area, requesting that it be known as 'The Hospital of Mary Erskine'. The Act ratifying its constitution was the second-last to be passed by the Scottish Parliament before its union with the English Parliament the following year. Three months later, Mary Erskine died and was buried in the nearby Greyfriars Churchyard, leaving the Hospital yet another gift of money. Her benefactions set The Merchant Company on a new course, which would eventually bring them fame as leaders of secondary education not just in Edinburgh but throughout Scotland.

The eighteenth century saw further large donations. In 1723 George Watson, an elderly bachelor, bequeathed £144,000 sterling to The Merchant Company. They were to use it to set up a hospital bearing his name, for the education of the sons and grandchildren of 'decayed merchants' in Edinburgh. After a series of delays, George Watson's Hospital finally opened on 17 May 1741 in a building designed by William Adam, opposite George Heriot's Hospital. Over 50 years later, in 1797, the next major benefactor came along. James Gillespie and his brother owned a snuff mill in Colinton and a tobacconist's shop in the

High Street, opposite St Giles'. He left £42,000 in all: part of it for the support of elderly men and women, and part to establish a charitable school for 100 poor boys. The Merchant Company were to be governors of the hospital for the elderly and the school, in time having sole responsibility for both.

In 1859 yet another charitable hospital came within the Company's sphere of activity. Daniel Stewart, from the country parish of Logierait in Perthshire, made his way to Edinburgh in his youth and began as a wigmaker's apprentice. Able and energetic, he soon obtained a position in the Court of Exchequer in Edinburgh, amassing a fortune as a result of astute investments. When he died in 1814 he left instructions that the residue of his estate should be used to build a hospital for poor boys who were the chil-

dren of 'honest, industrious and well-behaved parents'. Its rules were to be modelled on those of George Watson's, which he admired, and he wanted it to be managed by The Merchant Company. The complicated terms of his Will meant that they were not implemented until more than 40 years later; but then Daniel Stewart's Hospital in Queensferry Road was opened in 1855, in the impressively elaborate sixteenth-century style building designed for it by the distinguished architect David Rhind.

Meanwhile, The Merchant Company had been engaging in a building project on their own behalf. They had kept the Cowgate Hall as an investment, but they seem to have used it less and less. Gradually they disposed of parts of it, and finally sold the rest in 1784. Four years later they bought for £1,500 a piece of land on the west side of Hunter Square, just off the High Street, and there they built their new Hall. It was finished by May 1790 at a cost of over £4,800, including the price of the ground. They held their first meeting there in August that year, and then enjoyed events known as 'conversaziones' – in other words, receptions to which distinguished experts came to give lectures on subjects such as 'Merchants and Merchandise in Edinburgh in old Times' and 'Geographical Distribution of Material Wealth'.

By 1817 the Company had no fewer than 447 members, and the Master's Court felt confident enough to comment on all the pressing commercial issues of the day, both national and local. They protested against the Corn Laws, petitioned Parliament about what they saw as inequalities in taxation, kept a close eye on the development of the postal services, interested themselves in the construction of railways and canals, approved the abolition of slavery, and wanted the opium trade with China to be suppressed. In 1871 they even contributed to the fund raised for an expedition to find David Livingstone, the missionary who had gone missing in Africa. Nearer to home, they concerned themselves with the development of Leith Docks, complained that Edinburgh's High Street was in a disgraceful condition and subsequently supported the slum clearance scheme of Lord Provost William Chambers, which resulted in the construction of Chambers Street. Chambers also undertook a major refurbishment of St Giles'. The second new stained-glass window to be installed there in 1875 commemorated James Richardson, Master of The Merchant Company, while Sir James Falshaw, who would become another Master, was the donor of the very large and expensive Great East Window.

Meanwhile, the Company had become increasingly involved with its various hospitals. These were recognised as being comfortable homes where destitute children were not only cared for, but received an education designed to prepare them to earn their living when they left. As time went on, however, there was growing criticism of the hospitals. It was said that because they inhabited a somewhat enclosed environment there was no spirit of competition among the boys, who were characterised as being dull, apathetic and rather sly. In some quarters there was also envy of the hospitals' funding. By the mid-nineteenth century, only about two thirds of the children in the entire country

OPPOSITE.
The second Merchants' Hall, in Hunter Square – the building shown here as Royal Bank of Scotland (© RCAHMS Licensor www.rcahms.gov.uk)

BELOW.
David Livingstone, the explorer, by Frederick Havill (National Portrait Gallery, London)

who were of school age were actually enrolled in primary school classes, with only one child in 205 receiving a secondary education. (In England, the figure was 1 in 1,300.) Parliament was now intent on introducing universal education, and people were complaining that The Merchant Company hospitals should not be allowed to keep their large endowments. All that wealth was concentrated on far too few children – only 428 in all. Surely some of their funds should be put to setting up state schools needed for all the hitherto uneducated boys and girls.

Well aware of what was being said, the Company feared that unless they took action themselves, some (at least) of their assets would be seized and put to purposes beyond their control. Led by Master Thomas J. Boyd, the publisher and future Lord Provost of Edinburgh, the Company came up with a solution. They would convert their hospital buildings into day schools, charging a fee affordable by middle-class parents but also providing subsidised or free education for children of deserving families in financial difficulties. The new scheme was put into practice in September 1870, when they opened four large day schools: George Watson's College for Boys, George Watson's Ladies' College, The Edinburgh Ladies' College (Mary Erskine's) and Daniel Stewart's College. James Gillespie's, which was much smaller, would become an elementary school. They enrolled in total no fewer than 4,100 children, all but 200 of whom paid fees. Formerly there had been 23 members of staff in The Merchant Company hospitals. Now there were more than 270. Two years later, Parliament passed an act reorganising the entire educational system, setting up the Scottish Education Department and making new arrangements for funding and administration. In future all parents would be obliged to send children between the ages of

6 and 13 to school to learn reading, writing and arithmetic.

As a necessary part of this reorganisation, The Merchant Company in 1870 sold George Watson's Hospital at Lauriston to the neighbouring Edinburgh Royal Infirmary. The Merchant Maiden Hospital had in 1818 moved to a new building on the edge of the Meadows, and now the Watson's boys were installed there while the Mary Erskine girls were transferred to two large adjacent buildings at the west end of Queen Street. One was The British Hotel, and the other was known as The Hopetoun Rooms and had

been used as a hall for concerts and dances. Chopin had even given a recital there. An existing girls' private school in George Square was purchased in 1871 for the entirely new George Watson's Ladies' College, and Daniel Stewart's remained where it was. These arrangements put in place, The Merchant Company decided that it must move out of its Hunter Square premises. Not only had the hastily built Hall required endless repairs, but additional accommodation was needed for those involved in the administration of the schools.

In 1874, James Falshaw chaired an inves-

tigation into how much space would now be required, and it was decided that the next Hall must be in Edinburgh's New Town. There it would be located at the heart of commercial affairs, rather than among the increasingly dilapidated tenements of the Old Town. Four years later, an ideal opportunity arose when the City of Glasgow Bank failed dramatically as a result of a recklessly over-ambitious investment programme. It owned a large branch in Hanover Street, less than a minute's walk from Princes Street. Designed by David Bryce Jr, this was a handsome building with a spacious banking hall, strongrooms and a number of offices. It was put on the market in January 1878 at £21,000, but there were no offers for it. However, after private negotiations, The Merchant Company secured it for £17,000 shortly afterwards, and it became their impressive new Hall, a worthy setting where they continued to prosper.

CHAPTER 2

'A Great Educational Corporation': 1901–1913

With the unexpected death of John Macmillan in 1901, his predecessor Robert Weir took over temporarily as Master, for there could be no lull in all the urgent business waiting to be discussed, and a new Master was not due to be elected until the late autumn. Weir was energetic and experienced. His father had been a member of The Merchant Company, and when he himself was 22 he had married a 29-year-old neighbour, Mary Smith, the daughter of a merchant who had specialised in shawls, that vital accessory for Victorian ladies. Two years later he joined the Company, building up a successful business as a wholesale wine and spirits merchant and progressing to the role of Master in 1897.

There was much to be done, not least because The Merchant Company had really outgrown its Hanover Street premises. After a dip in membership numbers during the mid nineteenth century, the qualifications for membership had been expanded by Act of Parliament in 1898 to admit various new categories, including architects, engineers and surveyors, managing directors and bank managers. As a result there were now nearly 600 members, with a staff of about 20, ranging from Alexander Heron the Secretary ('a most polite and courteous official') to the

caretaker, Alexander Norton, who would soon take on the additional role of 'elevator attendant'. The elegant room known as the Hall, used for dinners and other functions, was simply not big enough now, for it seated only about 200, and more offices were needed for the schools' administration. Fortunately, the buildings next door, which at that time comprised numbers 10 and 12 Hanover Street, had been put up for sale in 1900, and the Company had been able to purchase them for the sum of £26,500 – about 1.5 million pounds in twenty-first-century terms.

A long series of discussions had ensued about the problem of whether to make alterations to the newly acquired premises, or knock them down and construct a new building to match number 14. The second option would be very expensive, of course, but it would produce a much more satisfactory result, and the Master and his Court were encouraged by the interest of a potential tenant. The North of Scotland Bank was eager to lease the ground and basement floors of a reconstructed building, and at a meeting with its directors on 3 January 1901 (presumably one of the last that Master Macmillan attended) it was agreed that there

OPPOSITE.

The domed ceiling of the hall in the Merchants' Hall (© Steven Parry Donald Photography)

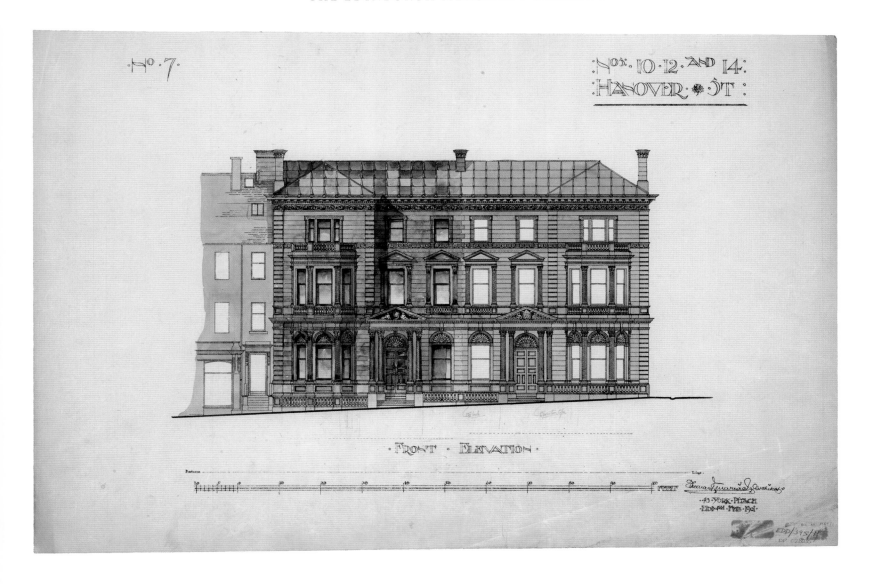

ABOVE.
Design for addition to the Merchants' Hall in Hanover Street, 1901 (© RCAHMS Licensor www.rcahms.gov.uk)

OPPOSITE.
Thomas Marwick, architect, by an unknown artist (Courtesy of The Royal Company of Architects in Scotland)

OVERLEAF.
The hall in the Merchants' Hall (© Steven Parry Donald Photography)

should be a total reconstruction. The decision taken, everyone was eager to move ahead with the project, and on 14 January 1901 the terms of the lease to the Bank were finalised. Starting on Whitsunday 1902, it would be granted for 21 years, with the rent rising from £850 to £1,350 during that time. The Merchant Company would install a hot water system, electric lighting and a lift. They subsequently agreed to provide carpets and desks as well.

The new building's façade would be the mirror image of number 14, with deep bay windows at its south end to match those on the existing north end. Likewise the door of the new part would be copied from the imposing portico at number 14, with its Corinthian columns and the coat of arms on the tympanum. To design the reconstructed building The Merchant Company commissioned one of its own members, the well-known architect Thomas Marwick, who had his office conveniently just five minutes' walk away in York Place. He had begun his career by designing a large number of tenements in the Marchmont and Bruntsfield areas of Edinburgh, and although he might

The domed ceiling of the hall in the Merchants' Hall (© Steven Parry Donald Photography)

not have been responsible for any major public buildings, he had made his name with numerous branch offices of the National Bank throughout Scotland. A dapper man with a small, neat moustache, he was notorious for his abrupt manner, even with his own family. However, as one of his students hastened to explain, his rather off-putting impatience was a result of the fact that he had such an acute and active brain. He also had the reputation of being a very hard worker.

In April the Merchants' Hall was emptied of its fine portraits and furnishings, which Dowell's Depository had offered to store for the reasonable sum of £15 a year, and the Royal College of Physicians of Edinburgh kindly agreed to allow the Company to use their hall for functions. Messrs H.T. and R. Montgomery, the builders, had sent in the lowest tender, and by the summer of 1901 they had begun enlarging the functions hall. The work continued throughout the summer and autumn. Even the tiniest detail of what was being done is recorded in beautiful copperplate handwriting in four handsome

ledgers kept by Thomas Marwick's office. These are preserved to this day among The Merchant Company Archives. Plasterwork was renewed, walls repainted, shutters installed, floors altered, plumbing work undertaken and an electric lift installed. By November the interior decoration was being considered. A Navona white marble mantelpiece was obtained for the Chamberlain's Room and the following January the decision was taken not to panel the remodelled Board Room (later known as the Court Room), but to take the less expensive course and be content with a plain wooden dado instead.

At the same time, Marwick was asked to produce a design for a mahogany Board Room table, five feet wide, 'with elliptical ends'. The Master would sit at the centre, with the Treasurer immediately opposite him. Marwick was likewise to arrange for models of the intended chairs to be seen by the committee dealing with the furnishings. There were to be 24 ordinary chairs, with the Chippendale chairs already owned by the Company reserved for the use of deputations to the Hall. Clocks for the Board Room and the Secretary's public office were purchased; in March 1902 it was agreed to redecorate the hall; and by 22 May, everything was ready for a distinguished company to flock in to the grand reopening ceremony presided over by Lord Balfour of Burleigh. As the *Scotsman* reported the following day, Lord Balfour in his speech gave a résumé of The Merchant Company's history before moving on to a stirring account of the need for improved Commercial Education. This was received with enthusiastic applause, and afterwards those present were served with tea and cake and had the opportunity of touring the entire building. They were particularly intrigued by the ingenious mechanism for locking and opening the doors of the strongrooms which would be used by the Northern Bank.

As early as the summer of 1901, Edinburgh Chamber of Commerce had expressed an interest in leasing part of the property, an approach welcomed by The Merchant Company as most appropriate, for the Chamber of Commerce had been established to provide members of the business community with a forum for discussing their shared interests. That same autumn, the Carnegie Trust for the Universities of Scotland had suggested that it might like to lease a suite of rooms. It had been founded that year by the famous industrialist and philanthropist Andrew Carnegie for the benefit of the Scottish universities and so it, too, was a welcome tenant. Since 1865 The Merchant Company had possessed the power to create honorary members, but it had never actually done so. Now, in June 1902, Carnegie, Lord Balfour of Burleigh and the former prime minister, Archibald, 5th Earl of Rosebery were all admitted to that position, and would maintain a gratifying interest in the Company's affairs.

All this was very satisfactory, but unfortunately it soon became evident that the stone used to rebuild numbers 10 and 12 Hanover Street had been of an inferior variety, and as early as 1906 a survey discovered symptoms of decay on the façade of the new building. Some of the stones had to be renewed and the rest treated with a preservative, but the problem persisted. Indeed, the reason why the elaborate pillared portico of the second doorway no longer exists is that by 1959 it had deteriorated so badly that it had to be demolished, leaving a plain entrance. On a happier note, the interior decoration of the Board Room was completed in 1908 when William Hole produced his painting, *The Reading of the 1681 Charter*, to fill in the blank panel in the overmantel of the fireplace. His fee was £180.

With their building enlarged and the necessary extra space achieved, the thoughts of The Merchant Company could turn to reorganising their administrative structure. The industrialist John Cowan, later knighted, became Master at the 1901 General Meeting, and was particularly concerned about this. When he made his retiring speech after serving his two years, he pointed out that the need to attend more than two hundred meetings a year placed an intolerable burden on himself and on the other office-bearers. It was true that in addition to the Master and Treasurer, Secretary and Chamberlain, there were also the Assistants, who in 1899 had been formed into an association; but the number of committees produced an extraordinary amount of work. To take just one example, the four schools which had originally been hospitals were administered by

Andrew Carnegie, 1835–1918, Ironmaster and philanthropist, by Catherine Ouless; after Walter William Ouless (Scottish National Portrait Gallery)

four separate Boards, each divided into three committees, making 12 committees in all. If the work of the four Boards could be transferred to the Endowments Board, Master Cowan believed that the number of standing committees could be reduced from 12 to three. It was not until 1909, however, that the complicated business of amalgamating some of the Company's ten different institutions and Trusts actually happened, by way of a parliamentary Provisional Order and after an enormous number of drafts, comments and objections.

Drawing upon their funds and investments, The Merchant Company had three main areas of expenditure. The important Widows' Fund had been established by an Act of Parliament in 1827, and it was still a major incentive for new members to join the Company, so that when they died their wives would receive an annual pension. Likewise, there was the responsibility towards the elderly and infirm. James Gillespie had not been the only donor to leave funds for that purpose; and in 1889, William Watherston, a retired builder and former Assistant in the Company, had gifted three tenements of shops and flats in Drumsheugh Place at Edinburgh's west end, the proceeds of the rents to be used for honest tradesmen who had fallen on hard times and were unable to work. Annual pensions would be paid out to those who were 'usually in the late afternoon or the evening of life'.

The third category took the form of expenditure on The Merchant Company schools. That involved a vast amount of work, and after the reorganisation of the trusts, a specific Merchant Company Education Board was set up in 1909, with members being appointed as vice-conveners of each of the schools. The transformation of the hospitals into day schools had been a tremendous success, the fees were indeed regarded by middle-class parents as being affordable, and there were always what were termed 'foundationers' places' for the sons and daughters of widows and others who could not manage to pay at the appointed rate. The need for additional offices for the administration of the schools is immediately understandable when the activities involved are considered. For instance, Robert Robertson, the dedicated Headmaster of Mary Erskine's, exchanged long letters with Alexander Heron, The Merchant Company's Secretary, every weekday during the first decade of the twentieth century, discussing everything from staffing problems to the poor quality of boiler fuel.

The Education Board dealt with a wide range of detailed matters requiring decisions to be made by them, and in doing so they always had to bear in mind the regulations imposed by the Scottish Education Department. They relied upon yearly grants from that authority to augment the fees paid by parents, and these grants would not be forthcoming if they ignored instructions. The Merchant Company Education Board interviewed and appointed the head teachers of the schools. They initiated and organised superannuation arrangements for teachers. They discussed the nature of examinations and the school books to be purchased. They approved the holiday dates. They arranged visits to the schools by distinguished people such as Lord Rosebery, their honorary member. They even selected the purveyors of school dinners and the window cleaners for their buildings. In doing all this, they were clear that they wanted their boys' schools to produce fit, healthy young men of high principles who would take their energy and values not only to the rest of Scotland, but to the whole of the British Empire.

George Watson's Boys' College still occupied the former Merchant Maiden Hospital

OPPOSITE.
Numbers 1–13 Drumsheugh Place, by Alexander Duncan Bell (© Steven Parry Donald Photography)

George Watson's Hospital, off Archibald Place (Courtesy of George Watson's College)

on the edge of the Meadows, and it was a very large school by any standards. In 1910 the total number on the roll was 1,240. The Scottish Education Department inspector that year had high praise for the teaching, especially at senior level. The traditional boys' school curriculum concentrated on Latin and Greek, but that had been gradually changing since 1895, when the universities had decided that Greek was no longer a necessary entrance qualification for the study of arts, science or medicine. Even so, Watson's boys were still keen to study the subject, classes in Latin, French and German were judged to be very sound and the teaching of both mathematics and science was highly satisfactory. As well as being instrumental in founding the Chair of Commercial and Political Economy and Mercantile Law at Edinburgh University in 1871, The Merchant Company had made sure that commercial subjects such as book-keeping were available in their schools, a Commercial Education course had been introduced at Watson's and woodwork was now provided for less academic boys.

Sport had always been important, particularly rugby, cricket and swimming – not only for the health of the boys, but because in the nineteenth century it was regarded as being the best training for military combat. Warfare was changing, however, and as early as 1875, Glenalmond School had set up a cadet corps. Now, in the aftermath of the South African conflict with the Boers, other schools began to follow suit. In 1903 Watson's therefore decided to found its own cadet corps, attached to the Queen's Rifle Volunteer Brigade, and it began recruiting the following year. Haldane's army reforms made it into the Officers' Training Corps in 1908, and when Lord Rosebery inspected the cadets during his tour of the school in 1910, he was deeply impressed. Afterwards he not only sent 'a beautiful edition of Scott's novels' for the Library, but invited the cadets to visit him at Dalmeny, his private residence.

Each year, the school head teachers presented their report on the previous session and took the opportunity of pointing out the successes of former pupils. John Alison, the George Watson's Headmaster, in his 1910–11 report, alluded briefly to academic achievements without going into any details, but he was proud to note that one former pupil had become Chief Engineer of the South Metropolitan Gas Company, while another had been appointed to a similar position with the North British Railway Company. Moreover, Watsonian Day, instituted in January the previous year, was now being celebrated all over the world by the Watsonian Clubs of former pupils, set up to promote internationally the interests of the College.

Daniel Stewart's had always been the smallest of The Merchant Company secondary schools, and in 1910 had 541 boys. Interestingly, its curriculum was now divided into two. Boys could either take the classical subjects or choose the commercial course. The choice, of course, was that of their parents rather than themselves, and Dr C.H. Milne, the austere scholar who was Headmaster, remarked sourly that the boys taking the commercial curriculum tended to come to school reluctantly and leave as early as possible. He was much more approving of the cadet corps, founded in 1912. In his 1910 report he observed that Major R.G. McDonald instructed his cadets with admirable skill, tact and enthusiasm, and the rifle range was in a good state of repair. Three years later, with fears of impending war, the Stewart's cadets were transformed into C Company of the 1st (Highland) Cadet Battalion, the Royal Scots Regiment, turning out smartly dressed in their uniform of scarlet doublets, hunting Stewart kilts and white belts and spats. Dr Milne was also pleased to report the successes of former pupils of Stewart's. One was now Professor of Education in the University of Sydney, another was Professor of New Testament Literature in Knox College, Toronto, and two were assistant lecturers in the Department of Education at Transvaal University College, Johannesburg. A significant number were making their careers in the Indian Civil Service, and two former pupils resident in Singapore had clubbed together

to donate £5 to set up prizes for academic work and sport. This may sound an amusingly meagre sum, but it would be the equivalent of about £300 today.

If Merchant Company boys' schools were taking the lead in Edinburgh with innovations in the curriculum and in the facilities they provided, the girls' schools were showing the way for female secondary education, not just locally but throughout Scotland. In the past, private fee-paying girls' schools had taught their pupils basic literacy but placed much emphasis on what were regarded as suitable accomplishments for upper-middle-class young ladies: singing, dancing, drawing, needlework and the keeping of household accounts. In 1876, however, Parliament had passed an act enabling the universities to grant degrees to women, although it was not until the Universities (Scotland) Act of 1889 that they were allowed to graduate, and they could not yet gain admission to Edinburgh Medical School. This was also the period when the Suffragettes were campaigning for votes for women, and the aspirations of schoolgirls were widening beyond the customary preparation for their role as wives and mothers. Given the lack of secondary schools for girls in the state sector and the inadequate funding for those which were being established, The Merchant Company can be credited to a significant extent with creating Scottish secondary education for girls.

There was still some tension between the old attitudes and the new, of course. At Mary Erskine's in Queen Street, class governesses were employed alongside the staff to look after the interests of the pupils. These were not qualified teachers, Robert Robertson the Headmaster said, but educated women with 'refined manners, good sense and sympathy with their pupils, over whom they exercise a helpful influence'. Although the medical

A classroom in The Mary Erskine School, about 1870s–1910 (Courtesy of The Mary Erskine School)

inspections introduced in 1910 showed that the Mary Erskine girls were noticeably healthy and well-fed, something of the Victorian attitude to women lingered on, with worries about the noise from carriages passing along the street outside being detrimental to their nerves, and the suggestion that the road should be paved with wood or asphalt to make it quieter. After taking a tour of the school with his wife in 1902, Andrew Carnegie wrote in the Visitors' Book, 'Surprised, delighted and impressed', adding that John Ruskin, the famous art critic, had said that 'there is nothing in the world that equals the Scottish mother in the tried perfectness of her old age', while the Marchioness of Tullibardine, a former pupil of George Watson's Ladies' College, was pleased to open one of its extensions, which was to provide classrooms for laundry and cookery. She hoped, she said, that 'the aim of an education such as you are receiving here is to turn out women', rather than imitation men.

Be that as it might, in 1909–10 the Mary Erskine girls were being taught Science, Mathematics, Latin and German as well as English, French and Drawing, to a standard praised by the Scottish Education Department's inspectorate. Robert Robertson's annual report for that same session proudly records the fact that no fewer than 23 former pupils had gained a Master of Arts degree, studying at seven different universities ranging from Edinburgh to Montpellier. Others were taking up careers in art, and Jessie Lawson, a former foundationer, had gained the British Institute Scholarship in Sculpture, valued at £50 a year for two years. Jess, as she preferred to be known, went on to have a studio at 33 East 56th Street, New York, and although she settled in London after her marriage to the English playwright, Howard Marriott Peacey, she continued to exhibit in the USA, winning the Widener Gold Medal for her sculpture *Belgium 1914*. Her white marble portrait bust of Charles Bain Hoyt, the celebrated collector of early Chinese pottery who had been the best man at her wedding, is now

North side of George Square, formerly the site of George Watson's Ladies College (Courtesy of George Watson's College)

in the Boston Museum of Fine Arts.

Meanwhile, the much more recent George Watson's Ladies' College occupied the handsome house in George Square which had at one time belonged to the famous admiral, Adam, Viscount Duncan of Camperdown, and had subsequently become a young ladies' boarding school combined with a preparatory school for boys. The Merchant Company had taken over the lease in 1871, but by the beginning of the twentieth century the premises were far too small for its roll of over a thousand pupils. Fortunately, the Company was then able to purchase other houses in

George Square, so that by 1911 numbers 3, 4, 5, 6 and 7 were all integrated into the College, the extension at numbers 6 and 7 being four stories high. Andrew Carnegie was invited to its opening, for he had sent The Merchant Company a very generous cheque to be put towards extensions and improvements at the Company schools.

There had, of course, been considerable disruption as a result of all the building work in George Square, and this accounted for the rather disappointing results achieved in the 1910 Leaving Certificate examinations. Charlotte Ainslie, the Headmistress appointed by

39

Charlotte Ainslie, Headmistress of George Watson's Ladies' College by Stanley Cursiter (Courtesy of George Watson's College)

embroidered velvet in the art class.

As well as its acquisition of additional premises at George Square, The Merchant Company funded a specially designed science laboratory at Daniel Stewart's, and in 1909 a fine new Art Hall was opened there by Sir James Guthrie, President of the Royal Scottish Academy. Even so, by that time the conditions laid down by the Scottish Education Department had precipitated a crisis. The head teachers of the schools estimated that in order to comply with the latest grant-earning regulations, it would be necessary to provide George Watson's Boys' College with new science laboratories, an art room for no fewer than 70 pupils, 10–13 classrooms, a hall for physical exercises and a workshop for 30 pupils. In addition, it would be desirable to have a library, museum, cloakrooms and extra lavatories. The George Watson's Ladies' College in George Square, despite its recent extensions, was in need of at least four more classrooms, and at Daniel Stewart's two more classrooms and a workshop were required. The worst problem, however, was posed by Mary Erskine's.

The Merchant Company in 1902, was a former dux of the College, a graceful and dignified lady who had studied languages not only at St Andrews University but in France, Germany and Switzerland. She aimed for high academic standards, commenting with satisfaction in her 1910 annual report that candidates had been put forward successfully in Analytical Geometry and Dynamics. Nor did she neglect the more feminine aspects of the curriculum. Cookery demonstrations were given to the older girls, and she encouraged charitable activities. Dolls were dressed in response to an appeal from the Zenana Medical Mission in India; 140 warm garments were made for distribution among the Edinburgh poor; and support was given to the Cowgate Jubilee Nurse. The school inspector was understanding about the Leaving Certificate candidates doing only 'moderately well' and gave high praise to most of the teaching, although he did criticise as 'incongruous' the stencilling with oil paint on

Because the Queen Street building was actually a converted hotel and suite of entertainment rooms, it had never been really satisfactory as a school, and now it was found to be structurally unsound. When a fall of plaster from the ceiling narrowly missed one of the pupils in 1903, The Merchant Company began seriously to consider demolishing the school and reconstructing it, and by 1908, the Scottish Education Department had made it clear that its usual grant to Mary Erskine's could not go on being paid until it was in a satisfactory condition. As a result, 16 Atholl Crescent was purchased in 1909 and the elementary department was transferred there, giving more space in the Queen Street building. Helpful though this was, it provided no permanent solution. Three years later, The

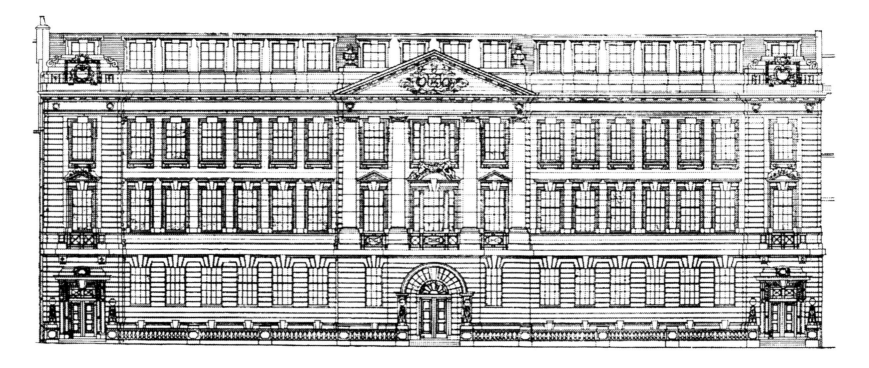

Hippolyte Blanc's design for the new Mary Erskine School in Queen Street (Courtesy of The Mary Erskine School)

Merchant Company therefore entered into negotiations with the Royal Scottish Nursing Home, which was at 69 Queen Street. Its owners agreed to move out to 19 Drumsheugh Gardens, which the Company purchased for them. This would give the necessary space for the east end of Mary Erskine's to be demolished and rebuilt.

Hippolyte Blanc, an Edinburgh architect of French parentage, had already had dealings with The Merchant Company, having advised them a few years earlier on how they could improve the acoustics of the Hall after diners complained that they could not hear the speeches properly. Blanc was a prominent figure who had designed many of the churches in the Edinburgh area as well as undertaking restoration work at Edinburgh Castle. In 1912 he was commissioned to produce a design for the new Mary Erskine School, and his drawings show a handsome building in the Palladian style. However, not only did the Company's Education Board

consider that it was far too large. It would also be alarmingly expensive, the total estimated cost being just under £46,000. So how could The Merchant Company pay for this ambitious scheme, when they had already purchased the extra houses in George Square for George Watson's Ladies' College and were going to have to make additions to the two boys' schools as well, to satisfy the Scottish Education Department?

On 27 February 1913, The Merchant Company's Finance and Audit Committee held an urgent meeting. Alexander Heron, the Secretary, and Henry Burnet, the Chamberlain (the two positions being separate at that time), had scrutinised the Company's extensive list of properties to see what could be sold. Some of these, like the cottages for the elderly at Spylaw, had come with endowments, but many others were the result of astute purchases made from the eighteenth century onwards as promising investments. By 1903, The Merchant Company possessed approxi-

Spylaw Street cottages
(© Steven Parry Donald
Photography)

mately 7,800 acres of land spread over five Scottish counties: East Lothian, West Lothian, Midlothian, Roxburghshire and Aberdeenshire. The most valuable were those where much of the land had been feued out, especially in highly populated areas of Edinburgh, where their value came to over £300,000 (more than £17 million in present-day terms).

The largest estate, however, was that of Peterhead in Aberdeenshire, which extended to 2,674 acres, mostly farmland, and at the end of the nineteenth century had a population of 12,195. Originally the burgh had been owned by the Earls Marischal, but the last Earl lost all his properties when they were confiscated by the government because of his support for the Jacobite Rising of 1715.

Sold initially to the Fishery Company of Scotland, most of his lands were purchased in 1728 by the governors of the Merchant Maiden Hospital, and various smaller additions had been made before the mid nineteenth century. The Merchant Company therefore became the feudal superiors of the town and its harbours, as well as owning a large number of the farms in the area. From the start, the Company enjoyed a very harmonious relationship with Peterhead, the office-bearers making regular visitations to see that everything was in order, encouraging agricultural improvements and even providing a large cemetery, opened in 1869.

The last thing the Company wanted to do was sell this valuable asset. In fact, given

the current state of the property market, Heron and Burnet feared that anything the Company now sold would be done at a loss. The sale of feu duties would likewise fail to bring in their real value, and would be both complicated and inconvenient. The only property that they could recommend for sale would be the fifth Merchant Company School, James Gillespie's. It was, of course, an elementary school, and it had become a problem. The Scottish Education Department were insisting on new, larger classrooms, but its endowment had from the start been very meagre. As a result, after much discussion, the Company had decided in 1908 to lease it to the Edinburgh School Board, and in 1910 they sold Spylaw Mansion to Colinton Parish

Council, who were anxious to open its grounds as a general recreation area. Likewise, this was not the time to dispose of any of the Company's investments, and so in the end the Finance and Audit Committee decided that they could only recommend definitely that the Gillespie's School building should be put on the market. Worrying though this was, Hippolyte Blanc's design for the new Mary Erskine School was accepted, and work began on rebuilding the east end.

On a lighter note, amidst all its serious responsibilities, the Company maintained its tradition of social events. There were the fashionable conversaziones and, of course, the annual dinners and receptions. On 17 February 1909 the members were enjoying a

OPPOSITE.
Roderick Gray, Commissioner and Factor of the Merchant Maiden Hospital Estates, by Sir John Watson Gordon (The Merchant Company; © John McKenzie Photography)

LEFT.
Master Sir John Ritchie Findlay (The Merchant Company Archive)

reception and dance, to music provided by Mr Dambmann's Band (which now consisted of 16 musicians) and by three vocalists, 'Mr George Campbell, Madam Kate Gray and Mrs Marion Christie'. Champagne cups as well as claret cups were provided at the Company's expense, and the whole occasion was judged to be a great success. The office-bearers also attended important public occasions, such as the levée of the Lord High Commissioner to the General Assembly of the Church of Scotland, and in 1912 they decided that they should wear special robes at these formal receptions. That should secure them a suitably important place in the processions,

always a matter of keen rivalry among the various organisations.

On 29 July 1914, Master John R. Findlay, proprietor of the *Scotsman*, would preside over the Annual Dinner. The menu was a delightful summer one, which included cream of lettuce soup, hot asparagus in butter sauce and 'strawberries *en surprise*', but the atmosphere can hardly have been anything other than sombre. On 28 June, Archduke Franz Ferdinand, heir to the Austro-Hungarian Empire, had been assassinated with his wife at Sarajevo in Bosnia and, the very day before the dinner, Austria had declared war on Serbia.

CHAPTER 3

World War I: 1914–1918

On 4 August 1914, Britain declared war on Germany. There was as yet no conscription, but young men flocked to enlist in the forces. Edinburgh tramcars were used as mobile recruiting centres, and many of the city's institutions appealed to their members to volunteer. The intended Merchant Company's Anniversary Dinner on 15 October was cancelled as being inappropriate under the current circumstances, and that morning Master John R. Findlay, successor to his famous father as proprietor of the *Scotsman* newspaper, spoke of the general pride in Britain's response to the challenges of the war. It was not the time for patriotic speeches, he said, but an opportunity for service to one's country. The Company must go on doing its work efficiently and quietly, and with consideration for the feelings of others.

We do not know how many members of The Merchant Company answered the call for recruits, but the number was probably very small, because many of them would have been middle-aged men with family responsibilities and large businesses to run. We do, however, have the names of two of the younger members who served in the Royal Scots, a regiment with which the Company had a close relationship. The first was

Douglas Alexander Lindsay, who had joined The Merchant Company in 1907 at the age of 31. He and his elder brother had inherited their father's grain merchant's business in Leith seven years earlier. By 1911, Lindsay was living in Newhaven Road with his elder sister, Mary Gavin, and another couple of relatives, but in 1913 he married. The wedding took place on 24 April in the Caledonian Station Hotel. He was 37 now, and his bride, Edith Maud Couper, was a year younger. Her occupation is not mentioned on their marriage certificate, so presumably she had private means. Her late father had been an accountant. The couple settled down in Pentland Terrace, Morningside, and their son was born the following year.

By then, Lindsay was a captain in the 5th (Queen's Edinburgh) Battalion of the Royal Scots, a Territorial Force battalion which had been formed from the 2nd Battalion of the Queen's City of Edinburgh Rifle Volunteer Brigade. The 5th Battalion was stationed in Edinburgh as part of the Lothian Brigade of the Coast Defences, but Captain Lindsay must have realised that they would soon be mobilised for service abroad. In March 1915, saying goodbye to his wife and little son, he travelled with the Battalion to Leamington.

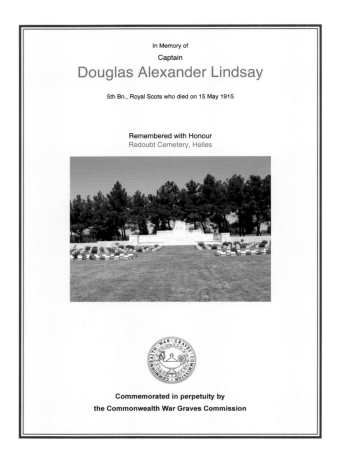

In Memory of
Captain
Douglas Alexander Lindsay

5th Bn., Royal Scots who died on 15 May 1915

Remembered with Honour
Redoubt Cemetery, Helles

Commemorated in perpetuity by
the Commonwealth War Graves Commission

ABOVE.
Captain D.A. Lindsay memorial certificate (By kind permission of the Commonwealth War Graves Commission)

RIGHT.
Advertisement for Mackie's Shortbread (Grace's Guide, 2007)

a new cemetery at Helles, and in that Redoubt Cemetery, Douglas Lindsay was buried. More than 2,000 servicemen of World War I are commemorated there, and his grave is one of the 349 that have an individual memorial. Back in Edinburgh, at a meeting on 17 June, Master Findlay referred sadly to his death. Captain Lindsay was, he said, the first of their members to give his life for his country and they would mourn his loss, but they felt proud that he had done his duty and they sent their heartfelt sympathy to his widow. She brought up their son in the house at Pentland Terrace, where she lived until her last illness 42 years later.

The other Royal Scot from The Merchant Company was Reginald Ernest Mackie, the son of J.W. Mackie, who had owned a large and very successful bakery firm at 108 Princes Street. Established in 1825, it had a factory as well as its shop, and in 1914 it was proudly advertising its shortbread as 'the Queen of all the Cakes. With the afternoon cup of tea it is delicious beyond words . . . a pure food of the greatest importance and value.' For five shillings people could even send for a sample tin, post free. Better still, the firm were 'Purveyors of Rusks and Shortbread to His Majesty

They then embarked at Avonmouth, near Bristol. They were bound for Gallipoli, where Commonwealth and French regiments were trying to force Turkey, Germany's ally, out of the war. After an unsuccessful naval bombardment against the Turks, the military authorities had decided to launch a land campaign from the Cape Helles beaches, beginning on 25 April 1915.

Captain Lindsay's military record notes that he entered the theatre of war on 22 March. The Allied forces were making little progress, and the 5th Battalion of the Royal Scots suffered heavy casualties. Reinforcements began to arrive at the beginning of May, but the devastating Turkish machine-gun fire continued and, on 15 May, Captain Lindsay was killed in action. The 2nd Australian Infantry Brigade had just established

ESTABLISHED ONE HUNDRED YEARS
By Appointment
Mackie's
EDINBURGH SHORTBREAD
Is the Queen of all the Cakes.
With the afternoon Cup of Tea, it is delicious beyond words.
It is made from the Finest Butter, Pure Cane Sugar and Flour of the Highest Grade. It is therefore a Pure Food of the greatest importance and value.
SAMPLE TIN · · · POST FREE 5/-
Price List on request.
J. W. MACKIE & SONS, LTD.
Purveyors of Rusks and Shortbread to His Majesty the King
108 Princes Street, EDINBURGH

the King'. Unmarried, Reginald lived with his mother, his brother and his three sisters. He had been educated at George Watson's College, and then at Heriot-Watt College. When he was 22 he became a Second Lieutenant (Supernumerary) in The Queen's City of Edinburgh Rifle Volunteer Brigade. In his spare time, music was his passion and also, like Douglas Lindsay, he was a member of Murrayfield Golf Club. The two men would probably have known each other well.

On 18 June 1914 Reginald Mackie became a member of The Merchant Company, proposed by Master Findlay and seconded by own his uncle, George Mackie. Two months later he was mobilised with the 5th Battalion of the Royal Scots, arrived in Gallipoli the following spring, and on 28 June 1915 he fell in action at the age of 30, leading a bayonet charge at the Battle of Gully Ravine. He, too, was buried in the Redoubt Cemetery at Helles, and he was posthumously gazetted Captain in March the following year. He had made his Will in Edinburgh on 26 January 1915, leaving all his shares in the family business to his mother, making bequests to his sisters and his niece, and asking that his Nicolaus Gagliano violin and Henry bow, gifts from his uncle George Mackie 'which have given me so much delight', should be sold, along with his Giuseppe Rocca violin. The proceeds were to be donated to the War National Relief Fund or some similar organisation. On 21 October 1915, Master Findlay sorrowfully announced his death to The Merchant Company, with similar sentiments to those he had expressed when Captain Lindsay died. As a member of the Lodge Canongate Kilwinning No. 2, Mackie was commemorated on their Roll of Honour, published when a memorial plaque to the Fallen was installed in their St John's Chapel, and both he and Douglas Lindsay's names are inscribed on the Murrayfield Golf Club's Roll of Honour.

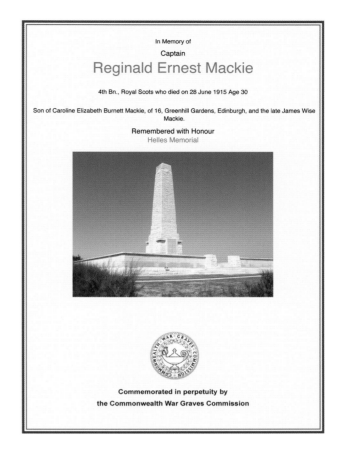

In Memory of
Captain

Reginald Ernest Mackie

4th Bn., Royal Scots who died on 28 June 1915 Age 30

Son of Caroline Elizabeth Burnett Mackie, of 16, Greenhill Gardens, Edinburgh, and the late James Wise Mackie.

Remembered with Honour
Helles Memorial

Commemorated in perpetuity by
the Commonwealth War Graves Commission

Reginald Mackie memorial certificate (By kind permission of the Commonwealth War Graves Commission)

The Merchant Company's interest in the Royal Scots extended to a new battalion which was created at the beginning of the war. On 12 August 1914 the *Scotsman* had published demands for a regiment of Edinburgh volunteers to be set up, and a month later one of The Merchant Company members, Lord Provost Robert Kirk Inches, announced the intention to establish a City of Edinburgh Battalion. The 15th Battalion was duly founded by Sir Robert Cranston, a former Lord Provost, who had interests in various drapery stores and temperance hotels in the city. On 15 October, The Merchant Company decided to donate £100 to provide pipes and drums for a pipe band for the new Battalion. Less than a month later, on 12 November, the pipe band played before the Company's Annual General Meeting, and Master Findlay made a speech, saying that he trusted that the pipes which they had heard in their peaceful hall that day 'might be for the regiment a solace on many a weary march and might encourage and entertain them in the day of battle and in the day of victory'.

Two years after that, The Merchant Company decided to donate a further £100 for a rather different sort of gift. In January 1916 the 15th (Edinburgh) Battalion had landed in France and were having to counter German snipers. That spring, the Company was therefore busy arranging to present the Battalion with eight rifles with telescopic sights. They had to seek permission to do this from the Master-General of the Ordnance, Sir Stanley von Donop, and were told that only four rifles fitted in this way could be given to any one battalion. They therefore decided to give four to the 15th (Edinburgh) Battalion and four to the 5th. The rifles would be made by Daniel Fraser & Co. Limited, whose premises at Leith Street Terrace adjoined Register House and who were contractors to HM Ministry of Munitions. Once the rifles were ready, they would have to be sent to the Chief Inspector of Small Arms at Enfield, who would see that they were issued to the units concerned.

January 1916 also saw the introduction of conscription, with the Military Service Act. This resulted in something of a quandary for The Merchant Company. Early that summer, 'a gentleman on military service' applied for membership. He would automatically become a contributor to the Widows' Fund and in due course, if he were killed, his widow would benefit financially. When he saw the application, the Fund's actuary said that he was unhappy about admitting anyone eligible for military duty. Contributions to the Widows' Fund were always made on a strict actuarial basis, and the Company had no power to increase the entry fee in spe-

cial circumstances. Should there be a sudden rush of new members who were married and who became casualties of war, the whole scheme would collapse.

Several further applications from men liable to be called up were held over until the Company could consider what should be done. Counsel's opinion was sought, and the advice given was that the admission or rejection of men liable for war service was an important administrative question rather than a constitutional one. Great caution should be exercised, however. In the end, The Merchant Company felt that the question of admission or rejection should be decided on broader and more sympathetic lines, not merely on financial considerations, and so they did not take their actuary's advice. Life in wartime brought many anxieties, not least because of the effect that the conflict was having upon trade. Captain Henry G. Speed, for instance, commanded the *Coblenz* of Leith, which was sailing back from Italian ports when it was attacked by an enemy submarine. A two-hour battle ensued and if an enemy shell had not failed to explode when it fell into the ship's coal bunker, the vessel would have been destroyed. As it was, the submarine was eventually driven off and the *Coblenz* sailed for home, but a severely wounded passenger died and Captain Speed had to amputate the shattered leg of one of his crew.

Despite the dangers, none of the Leith shipowners ever hesitated to put their vessels at the disposal of the government, and severe losses followed. In 1914 the firm of James Currie and Company had a fleet of 36 steamers and about 20 additional small vessels for local services. The steamers had sailed regularly to ports such as Hull, Hamburg, Copenhagen and Danzig, as well as to the Mediterranean and North Africa. Now, 18 of their steamers were sunk by submarines or mines or cap-

OPPOSITE.
Sir Robert Kirk Inches memorial in St Giles' Cathedral (Courtesy of St Giles' Cathedral; photograph © Peter Backhouse)

ROBERT KIRK INCHES, KNIGHT BACHELOR.
LORD PROVOST OF EDINBURGH 1912 - 1916.
FOR THIRTY FIVE YEARS AN ELDER IN THIS CHURCH
DIED 19th JULY, 1918.

tured by enemy action. Messrs Christian Salvesen and Company, sailing to Mediterranean ports, lost eight of their steamers, while Messrs James Cormack and Company were the most badly affected of all, losing 10 of their 11 steamers, which had traded mostly with the Russian ports of Riga and Archangel. By the end of the war almost half of Leith's tonnage had been destroyed, inevitably affecting the business interests of a significant number of Merchant Company members.

Throughout the conflict, The Merchant Company sent letters of gratitude to the government and to the military authorities for all that they were doing. On 15 June 1916, they expressed their deep sense of loss on the death of Field Marshal Lord Kitchener, who had drowned ten days earlier when his ship hit a mine and went down near Orkney while he was on his way to a secret mission in Russia. On 18 January 1917 The Merchant Company General Meeting decided that the Company should write to the Prime Minister, David Lloyd George, to assure him that he had their wholehearted support. That same day, they agreed to invest £50,000 (over £2 million in present-day terms) in the new War Loan. The conflict also brought increased responsibilities for Merchant Company members, and early on Master Findlay (who already chaired various important organisations) was invited by the government to become chairman of the Scottish National Housing Committee. It was being given the task of building housing at the new naval base of Rosyth. As a result, he was knighted in 1917, later becoming a baronet.

The Merchant Company was always quick to respond to changing conditions, and on 30 March 1916 the office-bearers presented a report on the increasing employment of women in the Edinburgh area who had been given jobs left by men now in the army. The women concerned were of secondary school and university education standard, and they were taking up posts in clerical and commercial work. By the middle of June, the Company had set up a scheme for encouraging this, and it proved to be a real success. Over 100 women enrolled, and a considerable number of them occupied positions 'in some of the best offices in the city'. A year later, Master William Fraser Dobie, owner of a large firm of painters and decorators in George Street, was noting with satisfaction that 150 women were now working in offices, banks and insurance offices. 'In some cases,' he said, 'the ladies have set up a standard which the male clerk, when he returns to duty at the close of the War, may find hard to equal.'

The war obviously affected the schools as well. James Gillespie's was no longer the responsibility of the Company, and the building had indeed been put on the market in May 1914. However, no one came forward to buy it, and the following year both the school and its grounds were leased to the War Office instead. A few weeks after the outbreak of war the Company noted that several requests from Dr Charles Sarolea, the Belgian Consul, had been received, asking for some of the Belgian refugee children now in Edinburgh to be allowed to attend The Merchant Company Schools. A Special Committee considered the matter. Aliens were prohibited from being in East Coast districts, and the number of free places in the Company Schools was restricted by their Endowments Order, but in the end Fernand Maas was admitted and spent at least two years at George Watson's.

There remained, of course, the problem of the Mary Erskine reconstruction. The old east wing was now demolished and the new one was slowly being built, but costs were rising, and it was not completed until 1915. In

February of that year The Merchant Company considered the possibility of moving on to construct the west wing, but estimates for that were far too high. There was the possibility of raising the fees, but the number of fee-paying pupils was declining, and so that was not a sensible option. The Education Board therefore decided that they could not go ahead and complete the entire building at that time. They were equally concerned about the problem of staffing at the schools. By October 1915, there had been numerous changes at George Watson's Boys' College: 'Messrs Shepherd, Shaw, Maybin, Cooper, Gerrard, Miller, Crowden, Gibb, Nisbet, Seymour and T.Y. Anderson left us for service with the colours.' John Nisbet was subsequently killed in action in France that same year, and Arthur Gibb perished in Gallipoli. Monsieur Naulet, a new French teacher, was called upon to join the French Army before he had even taken up his post at the school, and he was wounded shortly afterwards. Messrs Hay and Murray, the instructors in Educational Handwork, were now employed in munitions factories, and Fairley, the under-janitor, had returned to the Navy.

Daniel Stewart's lost one of its French teachers, too, when Henri Meslier's services were requisitioned by the French military authorities. The parents of the various schools were understanding when the French teachers had to leave, but some had a different attitude where German classes were concerned. In May 1915 The Merchant Company noted that it had received letters from parents at Mary Erskine's objecting to their daughters being taught that language by Mr Eugen Hinkelbein, who was a German. The Company were fully aware of the fact that he had actually been on the staff for many years and was married to a Scot, but to satisfy the parents they agreed that any who had complained could be allowed to withdraw

their daughters from the German class. Presumably as a result, there was then a noticeable fall in the number of pupils studying that subject, with 127 Mary Erskine girls taking German in 1913–14 but only 89 in 1915–16. At George Watson's Ladies' College, 96 dropped to 65, and at the Boys' College there was a loss of 17 in the same period. Rather surprisingly, at Daniel Stewart's, the figure rose from 35 to 51. As for Mr Hinkelbein, The Merchant Company allowed him to go on teaching at Mary Erskine's throughout the war. He eventually died in Edinburgh in December 1939, at the age of 81.

The Education Board sometimes appointed women to replace the departing male teachers. There was Margaret Robertson, for instance. She joined the staff of Daniel Stewart's 'as a wartime stopgap', and was the only woman teacher in the senior school until 1938. As Stewart's historian would write, she was fondly remembered for her energy and enthusiasm, running the tennis coaching, making costumes for school plays, dashing to the Cadet Corps camps on her motor cycle and 'teaching French with gusto'. At George Watson's Ladies' College, staff volunteered their services to teach French to soldiers and nurses going to the Front. Male staff enrolled for the Home Defence and female staff joined the Red Cross. Mrs Boa, a former matron, came out of retirement to act as chief stoker of the school furnaces, and when the janitor was called up in 1916, she took over his role at a salary of 20 shillings a week. Her daughter, Mrs Spencer, replaced her as stoker and assistant janitor, at 16 shillings a week, and was granted by the Education Committee a suitable uniform consisting of a coat and a hat.

George Watson's had made military training compulsory for all the boys in the senior school who were medically fit and, by mid-October 1914, over 100 pupils had joined the

territorial battalions. At Stewart's, 100 pupils were drilled every evening and a large number had already been sent forward for service. Meanwhile, the girls were playing their part in the war effort. George Watson's Ladies' College put aside its normal syllabus and pupils of all ages were set to work making comforts for the troops. They were then able to send a long list of items to the front line, to the many hospitals caring for the wounded and to the Grand Fleet. The parcels

they dispatched held pillows, flannel vests and knitted helmets, scarves, gloves and socks, books, currant loaves, jam and shortbread. In December 1915 each of the 80 crew members of the battleship *Orion* received a Christmas pudding weighing nine pounds, specially baked for them in the Domestic Science department. The girls raised money, too, in support of the George Square Bed at the Royaumont Hospital, which had been established at the ancient Abbey of Royaumont by Dr Elsie Inglis and was staffed by women doctors and nurses.

There was equal activity at Mary Erskine's. In 1915 no fewer than 650 knitted comforts were dispatched to France, and later on the school sent balaclavas and socks to Mesopotamia as well. Fifty-five dozen eggs were collected as the school's contribution to the National Egg Collection for the Wounded. The girls gathered sphagnum moss, which was used as surgical dressings in the treatment of injuries, and they provided toys for the families of forces and for children in Serbia. They also endowed three Red Cross beds in a British Field Hospital in Rouen, and raised £150 for the hospital by

54

LEFT.
Bomb damage to the west wing of George Watson's College, 1916 (Courtesy of George Watson's College)

RIGHT.
The bomb damage, showing the shattered windows (Courtesy of George Watson's College)

holding a cake and candy sale and concert. By 1917, some of The Merchant Company pupils were being appointed to more active roles outside their schools. Mary Kerr and E.M. Anderson of George Watson's Ladies' College were drafted in to work as interim assistants at Langholm Observatory, taking the place of two clerks on the staff there, and that same summer, at the request of the military and naval authorities, 17 Watson's Boys were employed for four months as scouts on messenger duty on the flagship at Invergordon. When they had finished, Lieutenant Wilson of HMS *Mars* pronounced himself to be very pleased with them, for their presence meant that seven seamen had been freed to go to sea, where their services were 'of much greater value to the country'.

By that time, the dangers of war had been brought home to everyone in Edinburgh when two zeppelin airships appeared in the skies on the bright, moonlit night of 2–3 April 1916. They had arrived over the Firth of Forth earlier in the day, intending to bomb the docks at Rosyth and the fleet. Turning away when the Royal Navy defences fired at them, they dropped several bombs on Leith, hitting a bonded warehouse and killing a baby in one of the houses near a railway siding. Another bomb exploded on the Mound, and seven people were killed in the central part of the city. Not long after midnight, one of the zeppelins dropped a bomb on the playground at George Watson's Boys' College, beside the west wing classrooms. The outside wall of Room 1 was blown in, all the windows on the front of the building were shattered, and the corridors inside were covered in dust, broken glass and smashed window frames. The boys, of course, rejoiced at the prospect of an extra week's holiday while the damage was repaired; but many parents, deeply worried, kept their children off school for some time afterwards.

At a meeting of The Merchant Company Education Board on 20 July the damage was described as being severe, and repairs were estimated at £1,400 (equivalent to over £60,000 in present-day terms). Stonework, joinery and the restoration of plasterwork came to £1,000, the windows all had to be replaced and plumbing and electrical work was needed too. In the end, the total expenditure came to £2,500 – but of course what weighed most heavily with everyone was the thought of what could have happened had the bomb been dropped on the school in daytime. The Merchant Company held consultations with the Chief Constable and were advised that in case of a daylight air raid, pupils should be moved to the ground floor or basement.

The number of casualties among the former pupils at the boys' schools was distressingly high. Of the 3,102 Watsonians who served in World War I, 15.3% of them in the Royal Scots, no fewer than 605 of the total number were killed. Among the many military medals awarded to them were three Victoria Crosses. David McGregor of the 6th Royal Scots was killed near Hoogmolen in Flanders, leading on horseback his section of machine guns. He was 23. Henry Peel Ritchie, commander of HMS *Goliath*, was personally hit eight times in 20 minutes as he sailed his ship determinedly into the harbour at Dar es Salaam, Tanzania, on a search and destroy operation. He survived, and lived on for another 40 years after the war ended. David Macintyre of the Argyll and Sutherland Highlanders earned his VC at Arras, in later life rising to the rank of Brigadier General. Like-

wise, more than a thousand young men educated at Daniel Stewart's served in the forces, a large number of them in the Royal Scots, and 215 died. The Military Cross was awarded to at least 19 of the Daniel Stewart's former pupils (FPs); three gained the Military Medal, and four received the Distinguished Conduct Medal.

As to the former pupils of the girls' schools, their war record is harder to quantify, for they were obviously not joining the forces. Nevertheless, we do know that Daisy Coles went to work for the 58th General Hospital Unit of the Voluntary Aid Detachment (Red Cross) near St Omer in France. The only George Watson's Ladies' College FP to be killed in the war, she died in an enemy raid. She was just 24, and she was buried in the Longvenisse War Graves Cemetery, three miles away. On a happier note, Elizabeth Smaill, who had been at Mary Erskine's, was in charge of a casualty clearing station in

RIGHT.
Commander Henry Peel Ritchie (Courtesy of George Watson's College)

OPPOSITE.
Master Alexander Darling by Henry Wright Kerr (The Merchant Company; © John McKenzie Photography)

Grave of Captain James W. Kingsley Darling (©The War Graves Photographic Project)

France, and in 1916 was not only mentioned in Despatches but was decorated by King George V with the Royal Red Cross, Second Class, for Gallant and Distinguished Service with the Territorial Force Nursing Service. This medal, instituted by Queen Victoria in 1883, was the first British military order solely for women. (It is now open to male nurses too.) Two of the former school doctors, Alice Hutchison and Barbara Cunningham, served as head of the Belgian Base Hospital in Boulogne and senior nurse at Limoges Hospital respectively, while another Mary Erskine FP was Welfare Secretary for 800 women munition workers in Messrs Beardmore's Works in Paisley in 1916.

July 1918 saw the second Battle of the Marne and the beginning of the collapse of the German army. The United States had entered the war the previous year, the advance of the Allies was successful and in October 1918 Turkey made peace, as did Aus-

tria at the beginning of November. On 9 November, Kaiser Wilhelm II abdicated and fled, and on 11 November 1918 Germany signed an armistice with the Allies. The war was over.

The following day, Master Alexander Darling presided at The Merchant Company's Annual General Meeting and put forward a motion which was unanimously approved. It said: 'With profound gratitude to the Great Disposer of events, the Lord God Omnipotent, who alone rules the destinies of nations, this Company of Merchants of the City of Edinburgh records its great relief and satisfaction at the cessation of hostilities . . . The righteous cause has signally triumphed and a great and outstanding victory achieved by the incomparable endurance and heroism of the Officers and Men of His Majesty's Forces on land and sea and in the air. Those who have fallen are tenderly and gratefully remembered with poignant but proud sorrow.' Master Darling's speech was poignant indeed. His only son, James William Kingsley Darling, had been killed on the Somme just three months earlier, on 11 August, at the age of 24. He had been serving with the 5th Battalion of the Royal Scots. His heartbroken mother wrote a short, privately published memoir entitled *Kingsley Darling: A Mother's Tribute*, and as late as 1932 his father would give £200 to set up at each of the four Merchant Company schools an annual Kingsley Darling Prize for scripture knowledge, in their son's memory.

Other parents also found some similar solace in commemorating their lost sons by establishing school prizes in their memory. The first such memorial to be announced at George Watson's was the Ford Trophy for Running, given by Mr G. Ford of Portobello, two of whose four sons had served with the 1/4th Royal Scots. They were both killed in Gallipoli on the same day, 28 June 1915, within

yards of each other. There were also, of course, the official war memorials. In July 1916, Arthur Hunter in New York had written to the George Watson's magazine, *The Watsonian*, suggesting that a fund be set up for the relief of orphans and dependants of those killed or disabled during the war. As a result, the Watsonian War Memorial Fund was established in July 1917, part of its aim being to provide a permanent memorial.

On 28 October 1920 The Merchant Company agreed to give a donation of £3,000 (over £63,000 in modern terms) for the war memorial, and the leading architect John Alexander Carfrae produced the design: a tall, pillared and domed arch, with the names of the dead on the pillars and on the walls of the apse behind. It was unveiled on 16 December 1920 by the Chancellor of the Exchequer, Sir Robert Horne, and the surplus funds would be used to set up a fund for the relatives of those who had been killed. Daniel Stewart's

favoured a simple obelisk 30 feet high, standing on a pedestal, with shallow flights of steps leading up to it. Designed by another Edinburgh architect, William Carruthers Laidlaw, a former Stewart's pupil, it was erected after a public appeal and has the names of the Fallen on decorative bronze panels. It was unveiled on 24 February 1922 by Lord Tweedsmuir (the writer John Buchan). The surplus funds there, too, were used to support relatives of those who had died.

Early on, The Merchant Company had considered erecting some form of memorial in the Hall to members who had died in the conflict; but perhaps because ultimately only two had been killed, this was never put into effect. However, with the return of peace, Sir John Findlay suggested that he, Old Master Dobie and Master Darling ought to present a handsome silver gilt mace to the Company to commemorate the war, as they had been Masters during those years. They decided to

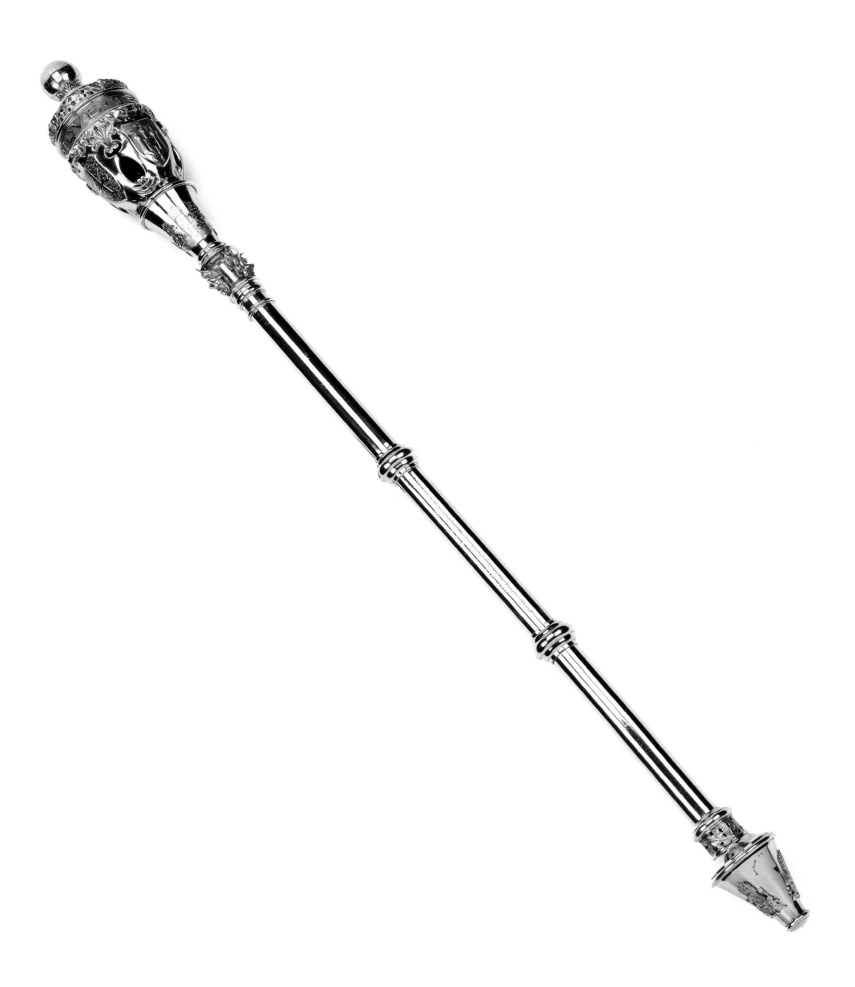

have it made by Hamilton and Inches, the George Street jewellers, with whom they had a long connection, and there was another reason why this seemed particularly fitting. On 19 July 1918 their genial and kindly Treasurer had died, and he had been none other than Sir Robert Kirk Inches, joint founder of the firm. He would never be Master now, but in its own way the mace would be an enduring reminder of him.

The mace was duly commissioned in 1919 and is 120 centimetres long. Now with subsequent additions, it shows the shields of the Company and of the City of Edinburgh. The sea unicorns and the Company motto also feature, with the globe at the very top. It is carried by the Company Officer in front of the Master and office-bearers on formal occasions. In June 1919, the Company also voted to give £100 to the Peterhead War Memorial Fund. These sad duties discharged, however, their thoughts were already turning to the future, and to regeneration.

CHAPTER 4

Vision and Reality: 1919–1938

On 25 July 1919, The Merchant Company's Annual Dinner was held for the first time since before the War, albeit with a considerably reduced menu. In place of the many courses enjoyed in the early days of the century, there was now a much lighter repast, beginning with clear turtle soup, moving on to boiled Tay salmon, roast lamb and braised ham, followed by the patriotically named King George Plum Pudding. A Milanese (lemon) soufflé came next, and that perennial favourite, strawberries and cream. Relatively modest quantities of sherry, hock and champagne were drunk, cognac came with Thistle ices, and port arrived with the coffee and was followed by claret. The menu makes no mention of any musical entertainment. Master Alexander Darling presided.

Originally from Lanarkshire, Master Darling had come to Edinburgh as a young man to join the family business of Henry Darling & Co., 'silk mercers, dress, mantle and millinery warehousemen' (a mantle being a sleeveless cloak worn by women). He married Eliza Rose Small, the daughter of another well-known Edinburgh outfitter, William Small, and he and his wife with their son and daughter eventually settled in 'Nordcroft', a large house in South Oswald Road. Not far

from Blackford Hill, this has been an area much favoured by Merchant Company members. Darling's large department store was at 124 and 125 Princes Street and, although it has long since closed, it is still fondly remembered by ladies of a certain age who used to buy their elegant garments there. The firm celebrated its centenary in 1937 by publishing *Princes Street Parade*, which would be reprinted many times. A delightful slim volume, it shows changes in female costume throughout the decades by means of 12 coloured fashion plates depicting elaborately clad ladies set against pen and ink drawings of various Edinburgh landmarks. Master Darling would be best known in The Merchant Company, however, as the benefactor of the Alexander Darling Silk Mercer's Fund. When he died in 1936 he bequeathed a large sum of money for the purpose of giving pensions to the elderly, under strict conditions. The money was to be allowed to accumulate until 1957, and then the income would go to Edinburgh women 'of good character', preferably unmarried or widowed, and to women who had been employed in the city in the manufacture or sale of ladies' and children's clothing. He also stipulated that preference should be given to women whose surname was Dar-

OPPOSITE.

One of a pair of silver gilt fruit dishes, 1933 (The Merchant Company; © John McKenzie Photography)

ling, Millar, Scott or Small, and to women born in the town of Lanark.

Despite the success of the Annual Dinner of 1919, there were no doubt the usual complaints from members who had been unable to hear the speeches properly or whose view of the speakers had been obstructed by the handsome pillars of the imposing hall where it was held. Hippolyte Blanc's earlier attempt to improve the acoustics by installing a canopy had failed to remedy the situation, and it was now suspected that the pillars not only got in the way of the sightlines but also made it difficult to hear. A more drastic solution was obviously required. Having the Master's chair opposite the entrance door and in front of an open space was probably not a good idea, and so it was decided to move it to a position against the south wall. That would mean that four of the upper columns would have to be taken down, but as they were imitation pillars and not the real thing, this could be achieved easily enough. The plan was approved on 21 June 1923, and while the alterations and consequent redecoration were taking place, meetings were held in Dowell's auction rooms in George Street. By January the following year it was acknowledged that although immense improvements had been made, the acoustics still left something to be desired, but it seemed to be an intractable problem.

Meanwhile, the daily business of The Merchant Company continued in the traditional manner. Master Darling chaired all the customary meetings of the Education Board, the Charities Board, the Widows' Fund, the Joint Committee, the General Committee, the Trustees of Peterhead Harbours and the Trustees of the Company of Managers of the Feuars of Peterhead. At the same time, he acted as a trustee of Robert Christie's

OPPOSITE.
Darling's Store, 124–125 Princes Street, Edinburgh (© RCAHMS Licensor www.rcahms.gov.uk)

BELOW LEFT.
Princes Street Parade, published by Darling's Store (Photograph © Peter Backhouse)

BELOW RIGHT.
Princes Street Parade, the fashion plate for 1922, against a background of George Street (Photograph © Peter Backhouse)

Bequest, Bathgate Academy and the Melville Bequest, as well as being a manager of Edinburgh Savings Bank.

However, in the immediate aftermath of the war there was in the country a mood of almost euphoric relief; thoughts began to turn to the future, and all things seemed possible. Edinburgh Town Council decided to consider the redevelopment of the city and, in so doing, they asked The Merchant Company to draw up a document giving its advice on the subject. It was hardly surprising that the Company was consulted, for, as we have seen, there had always been a close relationship between the merchants and the Council, and, in fact, in the eighteenth and nineteenth centuries there had been a succession of Masters who had been or would be Lord Provosts of Edinburgh. Now, the Company decided to set up a Special Committee to consider their response.

War had left Britain with enormous debts, and so its task would largely be to consider how to reinvigorate industry and commerce. The chairman of the Special Committee was none other than Thomas Marwick, architect of the reconstructed Merchants' Hall (because housing was going to be an important issue), and the leading member was of course Master Darling. The other ten members included his immediate predecessor, W. Fraser Dobie. The topics they covered were very wide-ranging; their printed Report, submitted by Thomas Marwick the following January, ran to over 50 pages and was sent to Edinburgh Town Council. This was intended not in an antagonistic way, Master Darling hastened to explain, but as helpful advice. Although many of its recommendations were too ambitious and indeed too idealistic to be put into practice, they make fascinating reading today, giving us a unique insight into the thinking of The Merchant Company members at that time. These

were, said the introduction, over 560 of the leading business men in the community, and 'the appointed guardians of over a million pounds sterling of capital, invested principally in estates as far north as Aberdeenshire and as far south as Roxburghshire, the whole free revenue of which is devoted to education and charitable purposes'.

The War had made great and organic changes inevitable, they went on. The Ministry of Reconstruction was hard at work, and the tremendous debts incurred could only be paid off by mobilisation of trade, intensive production, the introduction of new markets at home and abroad, the extension of existing industries and the creation of new ones. 'War has opened our eyes,' the Report declared. 'Our vision has been widened. We see clearer and better into the heart of things . . . National life must be quickened for we are on the threshold of a new world.' The Committee drew many encouraging comparisons with developments in England and the continent, and were even willing to admit that, however much the Germans were currently disliked, 'we must not be above giving them credit for what they do well' in the way of stimulating local industries. So what did the Committee believe ought to be done?

Edinburgh must galvanise itself, and become an industrial and commercial centre. Its strikingly picturesque and historical associations were not enough, and it was perhaps 'not altogether free from the easeful torpor and somnolescent characteristics of a University town'. Commercial Education was of the essence, and must be improved. Indeed, the following year the Company gave £15,000 to Edinburgh University towards the founding of a Chair of Accounting and Business Method. Above everything else, the Report went on, the area of the city must be enlarged. The authors did not have in mind

OPPOSITE.
The Merchants' Hall, showing the musicians' gallery in the hall, above its entrance (© Steven Parry Donald Photography)

the modest addition of a few acres on the fringes of Edinburgh. Instead, they listed 15 neighbouring villages which they believed should become part of Greater Edinburgh.

Some of these, such as Cramond, Corstorphine and Colinton, are indeed now part of the city, but the others listed included Penicuik, Lasswade and Dalkeith, which are not. Greater Edinburgh would then have had over a million inhabitants instead of the 320,318 officially recorded in the 1911 census. They would not, however, be crammed into densely populated slums. The idea was to create garden suburbs, with ten or twelve large houses and 'artisans' houses' occupying an acre of land. These new buildings must be characteristically Scottish in style, and built from Scottish materials. The creation of the garden suburbs would keep builders and architects very busy, and they would have to make sure that there were plenty of open spaces such as gardens with fountains and war memorials, where the old and fragile could sit and enjoy the fresh air. Space must also be set aside for allotments, and the Pentland Hills should come to be regarded as the playground of the citizens.

So much for residential areas. Industrial reconstruction was naturally seen as a priority, and the Report declared that numerous limited liability companies ought to be formed to exploit mineral deposits. Afforestation would be important, so that timber imports could be reduced. Car manufacturing was expanding significantly, and both the iron and steel industry and shipbuilding must be actively encouraged. Leith, with its population of 80,488, a quarter of the Edinburgh total, had most of its men employed in connection with shipping and shipbuilding, and so the Dock Commissioners' ambition to extend the harbour and docks, build a sea embankment and reclaim 230 acres of land ought to be undertaken at once. To

improve the health of the workers, factories should be single-storey buildings on the outskirts of the city. This was vital, for at that period 60,000 Scots were dying of tuberculosis each year. Fresh air and more spacious structures would help, and the activities of the proposed Ministry of National Health would surely result in a more robust work force.

A proper network of roads and canals for the transportation of manufactured goods would be of the utmost importance, with fast tram links for the population. The promised nationalisation of the railways could work a revolution in transport, as could current developments in air travel, in which Edinburgh might have a part. More electricity power stations were needed too, and it is interesting to note that the Special Committee at this early date was well aware of environmental considerations. A great benefit of electricity was that factories would no longer need the tall chimney stacks which so disfigured the landscape, they said, and pollution would be reduced. There were advantages for people's homes too, for ideally even small houses would come to have electricity for lighting, heating, cooking, and perhaps even vacuum cleaners, thereby reducing the need for domestic servants.

Above all, it was crucial that industrial harmony should be fostered. 'Employer and employee are interdependent. Let them resolve to live in amity. Distribute wealth. Let every working man become a land or a house owner, or a lender to the State, be transformed in fact into a miniature capitalist.' Large, unlettable houses could be converted into flats, while small, unoccupied shops in side streets could be used for housing until better accommodation were available. Local rates must be kept as low as possible and it was very important that the regulations for the compulsory purchase of land should be

OPPOSITE.
Leith Merchant Company coat of arms on seal
(© Steven Parry Donald Photography)

The Shore, Leith, in 1925, showing Thiems Ship Hotel, coffee and billiard rooms, perfumer and hairdresser, and R. & D. Simon, Ironmonger and Coppersmith (© RCAHMS Licensor www.rcahms.gov.uk)

simplified. In short, a Ministry of Local Development was needed. By way of conclusion, the Report listed in brief its 26 main recommendations. These were duly discussed at a Stated General Meeting of the Company on 27 March 1919, when one member pointed out some inaccuracies in the Leith statistics and another urged that anything suggestive of Edinburgh and Leith amalgamating must be omitted.

This was a highly contentious issue. Leith had always been Edinburgh's port and Edinburgh Town Council had almost entirely managed its affairs until 1833, when, as a

result of the Burgh Reform Act, it was given its own town council with a Provost, four Bailies and a Treasurer. It even had its own Merchant Company. During the Middle Ages, there had been an Incorporation of Traffickers who had undertaken the haulage of goods from the port up the hill to Edinburgh, and it had subsequently changed its name to the Leith Merchant Company. This organisation adopted a coat of arms very similar to that of The Edinburgh Merchant Company, except that the supporters were sea lions instead of sea unicorns and the globe at the top was on a plinth rather than on a helmet. In 1846, however, the Leith Trade Incorporations were disbanded and the Leith Merchant Company seems to have disappeared too. However, Leith merchants were eligible to become members of Edinburgh's Merchant Company, and by 1892, 60 of the 470 members were from Leith.

During the early twentieth century, representatives of Edinburgh and Leith Town Councils had sat together on the Leith Dock Commission, the Gas Commission, the Water Trust and the Water of Leith Commission; and now, soon after the end of World War I, Edinburgh Town Council suggested that there should be a complete amalgamation with Leith. Everyone was well aware that there was bitter opposition to the scheme, and so a plebiscite was held to gather the views of those who lived in Leith. The supporters of amalgamation are said to have numbered 5,357, while there were no fewer than 29,891 opponents. In spite of that, an Act of Parliament in 1920 amalgamated the two corporations and parish councils, since which time Leith has been part of Edinburgh. The Special Committee had, of course, wanted to see this happen, but otherwise post-war austerity meant that their grand vision of a Greater Edinburgh remained no more than paper proposals, and in November 1921 the Company's Anniversary Dinner was cancelled because of the very high rate of unemployment and the resulting widespread distress.

Despite the worsening financial situation, the membership continued to widen and the classified list of members for 1924 included an aerated water manufacturer, a chiropodist, a margarine manufacturer, a manure merchant and a photographer, as well as such well-known local figures as Jonathan Lyon of Lyon and Turnbull, auctioneers; James H. Thin of the famous booksellers; P. McOmish Dott of the firm of

Aitken Dott, picture restorers; and W. Birnie Rhind, the distinguished sculptor. The Company was also able to attract several highly important honorary members, one of whom was Stanley Baldwin, the Conservative Prime Minister. He took up the role on 15 October 1925 and was invited to a Special General Meeting the following month, when Master Charles Allan welcomed him 'as an administrator, a master of figures, a prince among industrialists, a lover of literature, an advocate of education and as a speaker whose addresses have a quality that excites and charms the imagination'. The Prime Minister

Stanley Baldwin, Prime Minister and Honorary Member of The Merchant Company (Scottish National Portrait Gallery)

in return praised the Company and its charitable activities, telling the members that their work was built on two particularly Scottish qualities: thrift and education.

The various Company charities were even more important than usual in these difficult financial times. Concentrating as they did on education and the elderly, they were not involved with the workforce, but they were certainly concerned about those too old to have a job any more. A list dating from 1929 gives the names of applicants for benefits from the Gillespie Fund. Although the Company had long since passed Gillespie's School to the local authority, it still administered his pensions to the elderly, and the people seeking assistance that year were mainly retired tradesmen in their seventies. There was a former Kirkcaldy moulder aged 72, for instance, who had an ill wife, had been a householder for 54 years, and was eligible because his surname was Gillespie. A retired marble and granite merchant had been born in Hull 73 years previously, but he had lived in Edinburgh for the past 50 years and his occupation made him a suitable beneficiary. Both men were recommended by their local church minister, and a number of widows also received pensions.

The economic situation went from bad to worse with the Wall Street Crash of 1929, which had worldwide implications and ushered in the notorious Great Depression of the 1930s. The Merchant Company had been planning grand celebrations for the 250th anniversary of the granting of their Royal Charter in 1681, but in October 1930, Master W. Stewart Morton announced with much disappointment that the intended reception and dinner would have to be postponed. The Company did go ahead, however, with a thanksgiving service in St Giles' Cathedral on 18 December 1931, when the minister, the Very Reverend Dr Charles Warr, declared in his sermon that the merchant must claim a nobler and more enduring achievement in the evolution of mankind than the fighting man could do, for 'commerce indeed, next to religion, has been the main civilising influence in human history'. The merchant and the commercial man were among the most reliable ambassadors of peace, for they could not prosper in disturbed times.

During the anniversary celebrations, Master Gilbert Archer presented the Company with a very important gift. Born in Leith on 6 January 1882, he had become chairman of an impressive array of companies, but always liked to be known as a Leith merchant. By the time he was elected Master in 1930, he was already President of Duke Street Evangelical Union Congregational Church in Leith, where he and his wife were regular worshippers. He was knighted in 1942 and died six years later. The minister's eulogy at his funeral gives a glimpse of Archer's personality: he had inherited from his grandfather a zeal for social reform and a remarkable gift for public speaking, along with his grandmother's sweetness of disposition and his father's ready wit.

Master Archer always took a particular interest in matters relating to Leith, and he also urged a current proposal to erect a Forth Road Bridge at Queensferry. With his encouragement, the Company gave enthusiastic support to the Queensferry project but, although the Ministry of Transport were in favour of the scheme, the economic crisis meant that nothing could be done at that time. It was shortly after he retired as Master in 1932 that Gilbert Archer marked The Merchant Company's recent 250th anniversary by presenting them with a splendid silver gilt centrepiece which would take pride of place at Company dinners. In the form of the ship which features on the Company coat of arms, it is 64 centimetres long and was

OPPOSITE.
Master (later Sir) Gilbert Archer by Malcolm Gavin (The Merchant Company; © John McKenzie Photography)

Silver gilt nef (ship centrepiece) presented by Master Gilbert Archer, 1933 (The Merchant Company; John McKenzie Photography)

specially made by Elkington & Company, Birmingham in 1933. Along with it, Old Master Archer gave a pair of two-handled silver gilt fruit dishes heavily embossed with a floral design, the work of James Dixon and Sons, Sheffield, also in 1933.

Another of his generous benefactions was to Daniel Stewart's College. In its early days as a Hospital it had a chapel, but in 1883 its stained-glass windows had been removed and the chapel had been transformed into a classroom. In 1914, however, as part of the

centenary commemoration of the death of Daniel Stewart, it had been returned to its original purpose and the interior was being refurbished with pews, a pipe organ and new stained glass. Master Archer presented the south window and, delighted, C.H. Milne, Headmaster of Stewart's, described how 'it glitters and glistens in effulgent radiance' in the morning sun. The chapel was finally re-dedicated on 3 February 1933 and the work was completed the following year, with the restoration of the ante-chapel to

commemorate the Fallen in the First World War.

Despite the Depression, The Merchant Company schools were continuing to flourish, thanks to their reputation for academic success, good discipline and affordable fees. Moreover, as Mary Tweedie, Headmistress of Mary Erskine's remarked, although the parents of her pupils were very worried about their children's career prospects, their own jobs seemed to be secure. An interesting analysis of the occupations of the fathers of

Daniel Stewart's boys shows that, in 1931, no fewer than 190 of the 590 fathers were actually merchants, with 104 designated as 'clerks, commercial travellers etc.' Few of them seem to have been affected by the current levels of unemployment. That said, the Company were unwilling to go ahead with the intended west wing of the Mary Erskine School in Queen Street. Certainly its architect, Hipployte Blanc, 'a good and kind friend', had died in 1917, but they could have found a replacement. The reason that they did not

LEFT.
One of a pair of silver gilt fruit dishes, 1933 (The Merchant Company; © John McKenzie Photography)

RIGHT.
Interior of Daniel Stewart's Chapel, before 1945 (Courtesy of Stewart's Melville College)

look for one was that the cost of demolishing the old west wing and constructing a new wing would have been astronomically high, and the Education Board were soon diverted by an unexpected financial crisis.

In 1919 the government introduced a minimum national salary scale for teachers, which was liable to result in a serious Education Board deficit. Urgent meetings were held with the Edinburgh Education Authority in the hope that they would make good the shortage of funds. Negotiations dragged on until 1922, for The Merchant Company were unwilling to agree that, in return for financial assistance, the local authority should have representatives on the Education Board and that the Company would consider reorganising its schools with a view to reducing their staff. After further discussions it was finally agreed in March 1922 that the Edinburgh Education Authority would contribute to the costs of the salaries increase and that they would be represented on the Company Education Board by six members. Recently, Master Sir Malcolm Smith had been concerned that the Company was losing control of its schools. However, relieved to have the matter settled at last, he felt able to tell the Stated Meeting where he made his announcement about the agreement that although 'they might view with some jealousy the addition of six members to the Education Board', past experience had shown that any members from outside bodies soon got into the atmosphere of the Company. Having seen the matter to its conclusion, he then retired prematurely from the position of Master to concentrate on his career as Scottish Liberal Member of Parliament for Orkney.

Two years later, The Merchant Company was approached about a very important project involving George Watson's Boys' College. The school was still on its site at the edge of the Meadows, its neighbours to the east being the various hospitals which made up the Royal Infirmary of Edinburgh complex. Indeed, in 1892 George Watson's elementary school had been sold to the Royal Infirmary, which needed additional accommodation – not least for its new women medical students. The Merchant Company had then added east and west wings to the College building to compensate for the loss. Now, on 17 March 1924, representatives of the Royal Infirmary came up with a new proposal. They began by speaking eloquently of the pressing need for expansion. The existing Maternity Hospital at Lauriston was far too small, and a new one must be close to the Royal Infirmary. They already owned a considerable number of buildings in Lauriston and a large part of Archibald Place, but these properties were individual houses, dotted about. Would The Merchant Company, they asked, be prepared to sell the buildings and the grounds of George Watson's Boys' College so that the Infirmary could erect its new Maternity Hospital on the site? After all, they pointed out, the school would soon be surrounded by hospitals: the Royal Infirmary itself, the Chalmers Hospital, private nursing homes, possibly a home for cancer patients, a skin diseases hospital and an institute for the treatment of venereal disease. They would purchase the school at a reasonable price, and The Merchant Company could then build a new Watson's College close to the school's playing fields, which were situated at Myreside, near the southern edge of the city.

The Merchant Company representatives were not impressed. Myreside was unsuitable. Certainly Watson's playing fields were there, but that was a different matter. It was too far away for the school itself, and there would be a grave risk that the parents would not favour this relatively distant position.

David

Solomon

The Lord is my light and my salvation

In memory of   John Ritchie Findlay

Merchiston Castle
(© RCAHMS Licensor
www.rcahms.gov.uk, Scottish
Colorfoto Collection)

The Royal Infirmary men retorted that neither would the parents wish to send their children to a school surrounded by hospitals. The Company brushed that aside, and suggested that the Infirmary should extend onto the Meadows. 'Not possible!' exclaimed the Infirmary. There would be a public outcry if they tried to build on that valued green space. In reply, the Company asked indignantly what would happen if they did indeed sell the school to the Infirmary for, say, £50,000, only to discover that it would cost them £80,000 to build a new school? Well, said the Infirmary, could they not build on their own vacant ground at Falconhill? 'Impossible', said the Company: that site was too small. Having reached an impasse, the meeting ended with both sets of representatives going away to give the matter further thought. Old Master Sir John Ritchie Findlay then came to the rescue by presenting the Infirmary with £10,000 so that they could raise their offer to £90,000 (more than £2.5 million in present-day terms) and The Merchant Company decided to sell.

Of course, nothing could actually happen until a new building was available for the school. The Company estimated that the cost of the new site alone could be about £200,000 (almost £6 million in present-day terms). They hoped to raise the difference by appeals to former pupils and others who had an interest in the school, and on 30 July 1926, at a Special Meeting, they approved a donation of £10,000 to the fund. Looking for a suitable site was very difficult, but they had discovered that Merchiston Castle, a much smaller boys' school in Colinton Road, very near George Watson's Myreside playing fields, was about to sell its building and move further out of town. The Merchant Company hastened to obtain a three-month option on the Castle and its all-important grounds, and by 26 October 1926 they had agreed to purchase the property for £32,500. The Royal Infirmary would be able to take possession of the old Watson's building in 1931.

A competition was then held for an architect to design the new school. The closing date was 31 March 1928, and in June it was announced that the winner was James B. Dunn. Born in Glasgow in 1861, he had been brought to Edinburgh as a child and was a former pupil of George Heriot's. He studied architecture at Heriot-Watt College and initially took into partnership James Findlay, another son of the original John Ritchie Findlay. Together they designed the new *Scotsman* buildings. Dunn had a fine reputation and John Keppie, the leading architect who chose him to design Watson's College, once said that 'like all strong men, Dunn was a good hater' but, with his 'frankness of conviction', you always knew where he stood. The cost of the new school itself was estimated at £200,000 and The Merchant Company Master, Charles W. Allan, was pleased, remarking that 'it was gratifying that the design the Assessor thought the best was also reportedly

the cheapest of those selected'.

Progress after that was slow. The Merchant Company set up an appeal committee but people did not come rushing forward to subscribe either to it or to the Watsonian Appeal. Sadly, James Dunn, who had been suffering from cancer, died suddenly on 25 August 1930, but his son Herbert, a member of his practice, was able to take over. There was no possibility of the Infirmary obtaining

the old school in 1931 as had been intended, but the masonry work of the new building was almost finished that year, with hopes that it would soon be wind and watertight.

By the end of February 1932 good progress had been made. The south block of the main school and the central hall were ready for painting, the tarmac was beginning to be laid on the roads, the finishing trades were busy in the Physical Education Department and

George Watson's College in Colinton Road (Courtesy of George Watson's College)

George Watson's war
memorial, in place at
Colinton Road
(© Ian Watson)

place on 22 September 1932. Prince George, Duke of Kent, a younger son of King George V, had recently become an honorary member of The Merchant Company, and Master Gilbert Archer escorted him round the school that day. The Prince began by laying a wreath on the war memorial, inspected a guard of honour and then made a tour of the building, pausing to listen to a combined orchestra from the Watson's Boys' and Girls' Colleges, who were playing in the central hall. Psalm 23, 'The Lord's my Shepherd', was sung, the Moderator of the General Assembly of the Church of Scotland said a prayer and then Master Archer invited the Prince to declare the school open. When he had done so, he was thanked by both Master Archer and the Headmaster. Finally, the Secretary of the Scottish Education Department expressed the good wishes of all the guests. As the *Scotsman* observed the following day, in buildings and equipment the new College 'must be the finest school in Scotland and one of the finest in the world'.

In 1935 the Mary Erskine Former Pupils Guild celebrated their jubilee with a splendid dinner in the Hanover Street Hall, which was decorated in nineteenth-century style with flowers and large fronds of palms. Prince George was back again in 1937 to attend the Company's 256th Anniversary Dinner. The Master by then was William Kinloch Anderson, the chairman of his family's large tailoring business, which he astutely expanded by introducing into it ready-to-wear men's clothing. The firm also specialised in highland dress, and in 1934 they had been given their first Royal Warrant by George V. William Kinloch Anderson had been a notably effective member of Edinburgh Town Council until his retirement from it when he was elected Master of the Company in the autumn of 1936, with the *Scotsman* praising his profound integrity, vision, breadth of

the masonry of the elementary school was complete. In March, Master Gilbert Archer described the design as being 'a masterpiece and outstanding'. Now that the building was nearing completion, he said, 'they realised the vision in the mind of the late Mr Dunn when he planned that great school'. A fire in the new biology laboratory in the north block broke out when a pan of bitumen being used by the floor layers caught light, but the insurance paid for the damage to some of the woodwork and, at the end of May, the swimming bath was ready to be tested. The large, gilded weathervane in the shape of the ship from The Merchant Company's coat of arms was proudly placed on the roof, and the 1914–18 war memorial was carefully transported from the old building.

The official opening ceremony of the new George Watson's Boys' College took

view and kindly common sense.

That year had seen startling events. In January 1936 King George V had died, and The Merchant Company had attended the proclamation of his son, Edward VIII, and sent the new monarch a loyal address. However, in what Master Kinloch Anderson would describe as 'one of the most trying episodes in our history', the new king abdicated that same year. Addressing a Special General Meeting on 24 December 1936, the Master remarked that although they would 'gladly forget the cause of the departure of the ex-King' they would never forget 'the life of service he spent among us and the devotion with which he discharged every duty attaching to his office as Prince and King'. Master Kinloch Anderson did not allude to the fact that daily life was also beginning to be overshadowed by fears of coming war.

ABOVE.
Prince George, Duke of Kent and Master Gilbert Archer at the opening of George Watson's College in Colinton Road, 1932 (The Merchant Company Archive)

LEFT.
Master William Kinloch Anderson (The Merchant Company Archive)

OVERLEAF.
Mary Erskine School Former Pupils' Guild Jubilee Dinner in the Merchants' Hall, 1935 (Courtesy of the Mary Erskine School)

CHAPTER 5

World War II: 1939–1945

On 1 September 1939, Hitler invaded Poland. Two days later, Britain, France, Australia and New Zealand declared war on Germany. On 16 October, German Junkers Ju88 bombers appeared in the skies over the Firth of Forth. It was a bright, sunny afternoon and people in Edinburgh, Fife and East Lothian had a clear view of what happened next. The planes attacked Royal Navy ships anchored in the Firth, killing 16 seamen aboard the destroyer HMS *Mohawk* and damaging two cruisers, HMS *Edinburgh* and HMS *Southampton*. They then flew low over Edinburgh, but they were pursued and finally driven off by Spitfires from 603 (City of Edinburgh) Squadron and others from 602 (City of Glasgow) Squadron based at Drem. Some of the onlookers thought that they were merely seeing a practice exercise, while others were convinced that their worst fears were being realised. Was this the ominous start of a campaign of aerial bombardment of Edinburgh? That did not prove to be so. Although there would be 18 people killed in the city during various raids, it would escape most of the aerial bombardment, because it was not heavily industrialised. Instead, the Luftwaffe would concentrate on Glasgow and Clydebank.

As in World War I, few members of The Merchant Company were directly involved in the hostilities. Some members, like the future Master, Iver Salvesen, were conscripted into the forces; but after it was all over, in 1947, it was noted that only two members had died 'directly due to the War'. The Company minutes do not record them as having been among the Fallen – they may have been civilian victims of bombing raids elsewhere – but do note that the lack of casualties was 'doubtless owing to the fact that the great majority [of members] have reached middle age before joining the Company'. An analysis of the Widows' Fund Roll made at the time showed that from 1827 until 1946 the average age of married members at admission had always been in the low 40s while the (much smaller) number of bachelors were typically in their lower 30s. Of course, the members were not immune to the loss of family and friends, or to the business and other anxieties that the war brought.

Master John Galloway was deeply conscious of his responsibilities. He had been elected in November 1938, by which time it was generally believed that war was inevitable. He was a former pupil of Daniel Stewart's, a justice of the peace and, during his long career, chairman not only of his family

OPPOSITE.

Barrage balloon over the River Forth (© Newsquest, Herald and Times, © RCAHMS Licensor www.rcahms.gov.uk)

iron and steel business but of various other important Leith companies including Henry Robb Ltd., shipbuilders and engineers, and the North British Cold Storage and Ice Company. When it became obvious that the conflict was not going to have a quick resolution, he and his Master's Court turned their attention to the safety of the Hanover Street Hall. It was agreed that the most valuable paintings would be packed up carefully, with expert advice, and stored in the vaults of the Society of Writers to the Signet, who had offered part of their accommodation for the purpose. If, for some reason, that proved not to be possible, the pictures should be sent for safe custody to the tenants of the Education Board at Spylaw and to Ladyrig House, Kelso. The precious 1681 Company charter, the first volume of the Roll Book and other valuable manuscripts were to be kept in the new vault at the Commercial Bank in Glasgow, one of the most secure in Scotland.

Even more pressing, of course, was concern for the safety of the schools and, as early as 1938, air raid precautions were being discussed. Everyone remembered how George Watson's had suffered bomb damage during World War I and the members were determined to protect The Merchant Company pupils from any similar danger. Some months before Master Galloway's term of office began, the Company had asked the Chief Air Raid Precautions Officer to visit the schools and prepare a report. As a result, all four schools were supplied with chloride of lime, which was to be used for gas decontamination purposes. The teaching staff were told about the procedure for dealing with decontamination, and were given instructions in the elementary first aid needed in such an emergency.

These measures were simple enough to put in place, but as the months passed, Master Galloway and his colleagues had to

tackle a far more challenging problem. Where were the pupils of The Merchant Company schools to find refuge if there was a bombing raid? The Scottish Education Department was insisting that schools must have air raid shelters. This was understandable, but the shelters would be very expensive to construct; and where were they to be put? Certainly the boys' schools stood in reasonably extensive grounds and in addition, because they were not in the centre of the city, they were believed to be in a less vulnerable position. The girls' schools were in the middle of Edinburgh, and there was really no space to erect shelters beside them in George Square and Queen Street. There was one possibility for Mary Erskine's, for it stood opposite the West Queen Street Gardens. The Merchant Company therefore urged the Garden Commissioners to have trenches dug, so that the girls could shelter there if need be. George Watson's Ladies' College presented an even greater difficulty. There was a garden in the centre of George Square, but there is no suggestion in the various minutes that it should be disturbed.

It was all very well to worry about air raid shelters, but would they provide enough of a defence? Towards the end of February 1939, the Company's Education Board had heard about a recent meeting held jointly by the Department of Health and the Scottish Education Department. Representatives from various private and semi-private schools in Edinburgh had attended, and had been told about the Government's scheme for the voluntary evacuation of schools in the case of an emergency. When The Merchant Company became aware of what exactly was being planned, they were dismayed. They were undecided as to whether their school pupils should be evacuated to the safety of the countryside in the event of war, but what really alarmed them was that they discovered that the Government scheme intended to split the big private schools into smaller sections, joining them with local authority pupils if necessary. The Merchant Company did not like that idea at all. It would be very disruptive for the pupils, and the parents would almost certainly object. They would be reluctant to pay the usual fees if the education their children received was to be the same as that being given free of charge to the local authority pupils, and, without the fees, the Company would lose a substantial part of its income for educational purposes. The Government scheme simply would not do for The Merchant Company schools.

The Education Board therefore met representatives from the Department of Health and explained their concerns. They wanted their schools to be treated as a special case and evacuated as units, so that the children could remain with their normal fellow pupils and teachers. Towards the end of May 1939, the Department of Health indicated that they could not allow any schools to be treated as a special case. The Merchant Company were not going to give up, however, and promptly wrote to Sir John Anderson, the Home Secretary and Minister of Home Security, protesting against the decision. Surely he would understand. His father, David Anderson, had run a shop in Princes Street Arcade and he himself was a former pupil of George Watson's and a graduate of Edinburgh University. At the same time they sent a questionnaire to parents and guardians, asking for their views about evacuation.

In July, the Education Board Vice Chairman and the Secretary set off for London to meet Sir John Anderson in person and put their case. When they saw him, however, their hopes were dashed, for he said very firmly that the Department of Health's plans were complete and that the Education Board's wishes could not be met. The Board

immediately came up with an alternative plan which they would later say had been suggested to them by 'a higher authority', whose identity they never did reveal. Possibly this referred to the Scottish Education Department or to the Department of Health. It is interesting to note, however, that the apparently unsympathetic Sir John Anderson would later be invited to become an honorary member of the Company.

Whatever the background to this new idea, the Education Board had already worked out all the details. The pupils would remain in their schools until some sort of evacuation arrangement could be devised. In

Sir John Anderson, 1st Viscount Waverley, Honorary Member of The Merchant Company (Scottish National Portrait Gallery)

87

the meantime, the Mary Erskine girls would join the boys in Daniel Stewart's building while the George Square girls would move into George Watson's Boys' College. Permission was then given for the George Square building to be used by the Edinburgh branch of the British Red Cross Society as their depot, while Mary Erskine's in Queen Street would become a First Aid post. Of course the schools would be impossibly overcrowded if the boys and girls were all to be present at the same time, so a double shift system would have to be put into operation. The boys would attend the morning shift and the girls the afternoon shift, then every four weeks they would change over. In the late spring, summer and early autumn, the morning shift would be from 8.30 a.m. to 12.30 p.m., with the afternoon shift from 1.00 until 5.00. In the late autumn, winter and early spring, the hours would be 8.30 a.m. until noon and then from 12.30 to 3.30. This was so that the children would be able to get home in daylight. What, however, was to be done about the severely curtailed lessons? This was not left to the schools themselves to decide. The Merchant Company Secretary held a series of meetings with the school head teachers in order to discuss the curriculum and it was agreed that most of the written work would be given as homework, to be undertaken during that part of the day when the pupils were not at school. When they were in their classrooms, the emphasis would be on tuition.

Some subjects would have to go, for there would simply be no time for them under the new regime. The teaching of Russian, for instance, would be stopped. Religious instruction was to be discontinued, although Prayers would remain. There would be no more music and dancing lessons for the girls, and there would be no shorthand or swimming at Watson's. These changes obviously had repercussions for the staffing of the schools, and the Education Board thought long and hard about how to deal with this. In the end, the instrumental music and dancing teachers (almost all women) were sent a letter warning them that the Company would probably have to dispense with their services. One music teacher had only two years to go before retiring, but although the Educational Institute of Scotland made representations on her behalf, the Board decided that it was not possible to make distinctions and, with regret, instructed the Secretary to tell all the teachers involved that they were now redundant and would be retired. They would be paid their salaries until the end of November and, if and when the opportunity arose, they would be re-engaged. Three of the catering staff in the girls' schools were also made redundant.

At the end of the summer holidays the schools remained closed, for the air raid shelters being built were not yet ready; nor had the evacuation problem been solved when, on 31 August 1939, the day before Hitler's invasion of Poland, the Government issued the peremptory order, 'Evacuate Forthwith!' The Department of Health's arrangements for the local authority schools came into force at once and, in all, nearly 176,000 Scottish children were evacuated under the Government scheme, with 120,000 leaving Glasgow in the course of three days. The Merchant Company parents were alarmed and dismayed. Less than a third of those who had responded to the questionnaire sent to them had been in favour of evacuation, but now there was a far greater sense of urgency. Deeply anxious about their children's safety and concerned that the Company had not come up with an evacuation plan, a number were making their own arrangements to send their sons and daughters to live with relatives and friends in the country or even abroad. In the end, over 800 Merchant Company pupils were evacuated, either under the Government scheme or privately, while about 350 others were registered with the Government's Overseas Scheme, which was sending children to Canada, Australia and the United States. By September, only 621 of the 1,263 Watson's Boys' parents had said that their sons would definitely be returning to the school.

When the senior schools finally opened on 16 October, the numbers were indeed considerably reduced and there were various noticeable changes. At Daniel Stewart's, for instance, when the boys returned, carrying their gas masks, they found that the air raid shelters had been built on both sides of the front lawn, auxiliary fire engines were parked in the playground and from the school windows they could see barrage balloons in the sky wherever they looked. The greatest change of all, of course, was the advent of the Mary Erskine girls, 'so that we became alternately morning and afternoon half-timers in our own house', as one of the masters remarked sourly. For many of the girls themselves, it seemed like an exciting adventure, as they investigated the quaint turret rooms and the unfamiliar masculine territory of Stewart's elaborate building.

As had happened during World War I, Merchant Company pupils were encouraged to take part in the war effort. Some Stewart's boys were soon filling sandbags for the hospitals, while senior cadets enrolled in the Home Guard. At Watson's, the senior boys trained as stretcher-bearers and fire fighters, in the following spring helping with agricultural work at Edinburgh University's experimental farm. In May 1940, the Forestry Commission asked the Headmaster of Watson's if any of the boys aged 14 and over might be interested in volunteering for summer work with them. This request met with an enthusiastic response, and by June there

were 90 volunteers in the forestry camp at Selkirk. Most of the boys lived in Selkirk High School, although some were in tents, and they started work at eight o'clock each morning, making brushwood paths through the woods so that the tractors could get around and pick up the trees felled by Newfoundland lumberjacks. That same year, the Scottish Education Department asked if the schools could help with the Digging for Victory activities. At Watson's, 730 square yards of the school grounds and at Daniel Stewart's the west lawn were dug up and vegetables were planted. Once again the girls' schools maintained hospital beds abroad and collected magazines, toys, tinfoil and sweets for a variety of good causes while the senior girls at Mary Erskine's worked during their holidays with the Forestry Commission too, as well as in the Post Office and the Land Army.

Meanwhile, The Merchant Company had not given up planning for evacuation, should that prove to be necessary, and in March 1940 they had a sudden breakthrough in their discussions when the Department of Health granted almost everything the Education Board had asked for the previous year. The schools would be allowed to evacuate as units, with their own teachers. The problem was, of course, where could they go? Early on, the owner of Arniston House, 11 miles from Edinburgh, had offered it as accommodation for an Edinburgh school, but it was too small to be suitable. In June, The Merchant Company head teachers travelled north to inspect various possibilities. Watson's senior boys could perhaps go to Keith and the juniors might be placed in Drummuir Castle, although it was not yet known if that large house would be available. Girls might be found accommodation in Elgin, but the Mary Erskine parents protested that it was too remote. On the other hand, they considered that neither Madras College

nor St Leonard's School in St Andrews was desirable because the town's situation on the east coast made it particularly vulnerable to air attack.

Although the threat of a bombing campaign seemed imminent for much of 1940, it did not in fact happen that year. Already many evacuees in the west of Scotland were drifting back to their own homes again and, in November 1940, The Merchant Company asked permission from the Scottish Education Department for the senior girls at Mary Erskine's to return to their building in Queen Street. Daniel Stewart's was far too overcrowded, and in any case the pupils needed to have a full curriculum because of examination requirements. The Education Board had to arrange for the Red Cross to leave George Square entirely and, luckily, since air raid shelters had to be made available there, Edinburgh University agreed to allow the George Watson's girls to use part of their medical buildings' shelter, while at Mary Erskine's the shelters had to be provided inside the building. Fire-watching then had to be introduced, to make sure that the schools were safe at night. At first it was mainly the staff who undertook these duties, but both the senior boys and girls later volunteered to take part, and did so – until eventually the novelty faded and it was again left mostly to the staff to do the night watch.

When Master Galloway retired in November 1940, he made an impassioned valedictory speech, describing how, 'One by one, our friends across the channel have fallen under the yoke of the tyrant and swiftly and inexorably he has swept nearer and nearer to the citadel of our empire. Today he is storming mercilessly at the gates with the cruellest weapon that the misapplied ingenuity of man has ever devised [aerial bombardment]. I am no military strategist, but as a plain business man I am neither impressed nor am I depressed by the sight of the territorial successes which the enemy has gained . . . For the moment we fight alone, but we have no fear . . . In one brief year, gentlemen, we have become a changed people. Here we are, gladly, cheerfully paying heavy taxes, counting not the cost, gladly opening the doors of our houses to total strangers, sending our children to safety to our far-flung dominions across the sea and, in a thousand ways, living as we knew not how to live a year ago.'

A week earlier one of the Company's honorary members, the Prime Minister Neville Chamberlain, had died. His successor, Winston Churchill, was approached and accepted the invitation to take his place. Not surprisingly, Churchill had no time to visit the Merchants' Hall, and indeed it was not until 14 February 1950 that he added his small, neat signature to the Roll during a visit to Edinburgh, when Master Iver Salvesen took the book to the North British Hotel where he was staying. In October 1941, John Gilbert Winant was also given honorary membership. A Republican politician, he was the United States ambassador to Great Britain for most of the War. After visiting the Merchants' Hall, he wrote to thank the Company for his reception in what he described as 'a kindly, homely, privileged and cultural atmosphere'. In 1943, another four honorary members followed: the Earl of Woolton, Minister of Food; Sir Thomas Holland, Principal of Edinburgh University; Field Marshal Jan Christiaan Smuts, Prime Minister of South Africa; and the 1st Viscount Waverley, who was none other than Sir John Anderson. The willingness of such eminent men to associate themselves with the Company was a sure sign of its prestige and a very helpful encouragement to the morale of members in such difficult times. No further honorary members were created during the War.

OPPOSITE.
Neville Chamberlain, Honorary Member of The Merchant Company (Scottish National Portrait Gallery)

Meanwhile, Master Galloway had been succeeded by David Pentland. A wool merchant, born in Renfrew, he had settled in Leith. To his great disappointment he was unable to carry out his responsibilities as Master, for he was already seriously ill with aplastic anaemia and he died in office on 20 July 1941, at the age of 71. The Treasurer, John Letham White, had taken over many of his duties and in October he was formally nominated as the next Master. In his middle fifties now, White was a civil engineer who had formerly served as a captain in the Royal Engineers during World War I. A purposeful and energetic man of strong opinions, he would later be awarded a CBE for political and public services. Master White gave very vigorous leadership to the Company and he was determined to make positive plans for the future. In 1943, with his encouragement, the Education Board purchased an elegant Georgian house at 58 St Alban's Road, once used as a private school, to accommodate the George Watson's Ladies' College nursery classes and

some elementary classes. It cost £2,300, with an additional £900 to £1,200 set aside for alterations and furniture.

That same spring, Master White was pleased to report that the Company had also purchased Dean Park House on Queensferry Road, close to Daniel Stewart's. A handsome, spacious mansion with fine views of the River Forth, it had belonged to Lord Salvesen, the High Court judge. He had extended its grounds by leasing two and a half acres of land beside it from The Merchant Company. A month after Lord Salvesen's death in February 1942, his trustees asked whether the Company would be interested in purchasing the house. This was very opportune, for at the beginning of the war they had been forced to abandon plans to build an extension to Stewart's. Master White was of the opinion that Dean Park House would make a suitable nursery school for Stewart's, and the following year it was duly purchased at a cost of £3,000. Unfortunately, only two months later, Master White was wryly passing on the news that the

OPPOSITE.
Winston Churchill, Honorary Member of The Merchant Company (Scottish National Portrait Gallery)

RIGHT.
Master David Pentland (The Merchant Company Archive)

FAR RIGHT.
Master John L. White (The Merchant Company Archive)

George Watson's Ladies' College at 58 St Alban's Road (Courtesy of George Watson's College)

building had just been requisitioned by the military authorities. However, as he remarked philosophically, 'this difficulty should not always be with us'.

Property purchases apart, Master White was also busy with a questionnaire sent to the Company by the Lord Provost, Sir Will Y. Darling, nephew of Old Master Alexander Darling and a member of the Company. The subject of the questionnaire was the future development of Edinburgh, and Master White chaired the discussions of the Special Committee set up for the purpose, signing the eventual report on 22 July 1943. In a way, it makes an interesting contrast with the vision for the future of Edinburgh expressed by the Company at the end of World War I. That had been composed in a mood of euphoric relief at the return of peace, and its suggestions had been highly imaginative and wide-ranging. The new report, written in wartime and constrained by the eight ques-

tions being asked, ran to only seven pages, and rather than envisaging a vastly enlarged Edinburgh, it concentrated on ideas for improving the existing city. Its views on the importance of industry and commerce were, however, predictably unchanged, the report remarking briskly that 'Edinburgh cannot live on culture alone . . . Industry must be developed.' Lord Nuffield's Morris car works in Oxford had shown that this could be done without spoiling a city or taking away from its beauty. Existing industries should therefore be expanded and new ones introduced, preferably of the light or medium variety, such as the manufacture of breakfast cereals, plastics, glass and crystal ware, boots and shoes, motor cars and cycles, fine furniture and mass-produced doors and windows from timber imported into Leith.

The authors then turned to the subject of housing. Unlike their predecessors, their concern was not primarily with low-density

Dean Park House (Courtesy of Stewart's Melville College)

new housing. The priority, they said, was to demolish the slum properties in Leith and replace them with modern houses. Ship-building would inevitably be important because of the anticipated revival of trade between Leith and the continent when peace came, and the need to replace ships lost during the War. It would be best, therefore, if the workers could live nearby. Elsewhere, large blocks of residential flats for workers, along the lines of those built in Stockholm and Vienna, should be constructed and could have shared dining and recreational facilities with well-kept communal gardens, drying greens and children's playgrounds.

Wherever possible, buildings of real historical significance should be preserved, but the welfare of the community must come first. A lot of old buildings, like Huntly House and Gladstone's Land, were deemed to be unsuitable for domestic life and were best fitted for use as museums or meeting places

for societies. The Town Planning Department should also undertake a survey of the entire city of Edinburgh to see which areas could be cleared of housing altogether and used instead for industrial purposes, while industrial estates should be established on the outskirts of the city. Of course, parks and official open spaces should not be built upon but should continue to act as lungs for the city. The creation of satellite towns, which had apparently been suggested in the questionnaire, was not desirable. Edinburgh had enough to do without taking subsidiary towns under its wing.

As for transport, an airport for Edinburgh ought to be established, and assistance might be given to Edinburgh University to found a Department of Aeronautical Engineering. The current scheme for a ring road was useful, but radial roads leading from it were judged to be impractical because of the hilly nature of the countryside. It was proving impossible to

repair tram tracks during the War as fast as they were being worn down, and so a trolley bus service should be set up instead as soon as the War was over. Bus routes would have to be expanded too. Asked about national and local government buildings, the authors of the Report felt that these ought to be centralised if possible, with all the municipal buildings located in the High Street, already the site of the City Chambers. Tourist traffic could be considerably developed. At the moment good hotel accommodation was lacking, and so a first-class hotel on the lines of the Cumberland Hotel in London would be a great attraction and a source of revenue. There was also a lack of good restaurants, and people wishing to open such businesses should be encouraged, particularly those prepared to supply meals on Sundays.

There could be organised entertainments for tourists, too: 'good class concerts and drama attract visitors to other towns and would prove popular in Edinburgh. A good municipal orchestra in the Capital of Scotland is surely not outwith the bounds of possibility.' Pleasure steamers might be re-established on the River Forth, although that, of course, would mean the erection of a pier at Portobello. The banks of the Water of Leith should be made accessible to the public from Colinton to the Forth, and the suburban railway ought to be electrified. The railway through Princes Street Gardens might be covered in, to allow people 'to listen to the bands there in peace'. In all future developments, steps must be taken to cut down the smoke nuisance and new houses should be smokeless.

Finally, the report made some general observations not covered by the actual questions asked. A road bridge across the Forth at South Queensferry and a Forth and Clyde ship canal were both long overdue and light and airy schools of modern design must be built throughout Edinburgh, with playing fields beside them. Primary schools should not have more than 600 pupils, purely secondary schools would have to be developed as required and so too would nursery schools and technical schools. 'The Merchant Company Education Board is prepared to play its part in the provision of new schools' is the last sentence in the Report, which was printed and passed to the Town Council's Advisory Committee on City Development in October. Master White took up the theme of school buildings again when he made his valedictory speech to the Education Board at a Stated Meeting on 28 October 1943, observing that the outstanding debt for the new George Watson's Boys' College was about £90,000 (approximately £2.5 million pounds in present-day terms) and the Company could not therefore afford to take on much more than the schools' maintenance costs in the foreseeable future. However, he emphasised that in his view, the continuation of the Company's Education Board would only be tolerated by the Government and by the public if the school buildings were modern in design and equipment. Were suitable financial arrangements forthcoming, new buildings would be needed for the other three schools. Rather than putting up an extension to the east of Daniel Stewart's, as had been intended, they could utilise the two and a half acres formerly leased to Lord Salvesen. A new building there would probably cost at least £50,000.

George Watson's girls' school also required more accommodation. Some years earlier, the school had acquired playing fields at Liberton, and now a 12-acre site overlooking them had become available. Master White had consulted his friend Thomas Tait, 'probably the most eminent architect in Britain today', and Mr Tait had drawn up small-scale plans to show how a building for 1,000 or 1,300 pupils could be erected there, at a total

OPPOSITE.
Sir Will Y. Darling, Lord Provost of Edinburgh (Scottish National Portrait Gallery)

cost of £154,000. Mary Erskine's had approximately the same number of pupils, and a new building for them could be put up on the Company schools' playing fields at Inverleith. Despite the War, Master White was convinced that the Education Board should prepare plans for these new buildings 'at the very earliest moment', and they must be of modern design and good materials – definitely not, he said, the combination of natural and artificial stone used in the George Watson's Boys' College building. As the total cost of all this would be £420,000, money would have to be borrowed to augment the Education Board's income from endowments, parents' fees and Government grants, and it could be spread over anything up to 30 years.

Master White likewise took the opportunity of touching upon what he saw as the deficiencies of The Merchant Company teaching staff. Justifying the regrettable but necessary decision to make redundancies when the shift system was introduced, he went on to say that the time had come to revise teacher training. In his opinion, teachers had become too circumscribed in their experience, and their outlook on world affairs was not as broad as it should be. They ought to be allowed to work 'in the outside world' for specific periods, in the fields of commerce, accounting and banking. Every second or third year, they should study their own particular subject in the long vacation. How these suggestions were received by the teachers is not recorded but, invigorated by such positive and imaginative thoughts for the future, the Education Board set up a special Daniel Stewart's College Advisory Committee. This reported the following March, advising that a new Junior School was necessary, and gave details of all the facilities required.

Despite the restrictions, the rationing of

food, the need for clothing coupons and the uncertainty about the future, The Merchant Company remained in a good condition throughout the war years. The membership numbers had fallen to a new low of 520, it was true, but when Master White visited the various properties in Edinburgh, Aberdeenshire, the Lothians and Roxburghshire in 1943 he found them all, as far as he could tell, prosperous and in a good state of repair. The Company's finances were sound and the productive capital, which had amounted to £51,405 4s 4d on 1 September 1939, had risen to £55,181 11s 4d on the corresponding date in 1946. This satisfactory state of affairs was, however, overshadowed by the losses suffered by the former pupils of the Company schools. Of a total 1,822 Watsonians serving with the forces, 202 were killed or died on active service. Eighty of the Stewart's former pupils were among the Fallen, but among those who survived was Donald Cruikshank VC.

The first Watson's casualty was Sandy Bathgate, aged 21, missing, presumed dead on 6 September 1939 after a bombing raid. Another who died was Raymond Valvona, only son of a member of the well-known Valvona and Crolla family. He had trained at Leith Nautical College, and was only 16 when he made his first voyage on a tanker to Trinidad. It was torpedoed on the way home, just a day's journey from Leith. Six of the crew of 39 were saved, but Raymond was among the dead. In both of the boys' schools, a significant number of those who perished were in the Royal Air Force. As before, it is difficult to compile casualty figures for the girls' schools, but we know about Ruby Grierson, a former member of staff at George Watson's Ladies' College and sister of the pioneering documentary filmmaker John Grierson. She was travelling as a film maker with *The City of Benares*, taking British evacuees

Master John S. Blair
(The Merchant Company
Archive)

from Liverpool to Montreal, when it too was torpedoed and she drowned.

John S. Blair, who succeeded Master White in 1943, was a gentler character than his outspoken predecessor. The owner of his family drapery business, he was, said Lord Provost Darling, 'the most unostentatious of men', who had never sought any prominent position for himself. It was Master Blair, however, who had the satisfaction of convening a special meeting on 17 May 1945 to tell the members that, 'With profound gratitude to Divine Providence, The Company of Merchants of the City of Edinburgh records its joy and satisfaction at the cessation of the War in Europe and the complete victory of the just cause of the Allied Nations after five years and eight months of supreme effort, sacrifice and constant courage.' He traced the events of these past years and months, paying tribute to the leadership of King George VI, Queen Elizabeth, Winston Churchill and others, and noting with sadness the casualties among the former pupils of The Merchant Company Schools. However, 'secure, then, in the righteousness of our cause, we may look forward with confidence to the future'.

CHAPTER 6

Royal Connections, Fraser Homes and Ravelston: 1946–1964

In 1948, Master William Drummond and The Merchant Company were busily making plans for a very special event which was particularly welcome during the continuing years of austerity that followed World War II. On 20 November 1947 King George VI's elder daughter, Princess Elizabeth, had married Prince Philip, Duke of Edinburgh, and shortly afterwards the young royal couple agreed to become honorary members of The Merchant Company. The admission ceremony took place on 3 March 1949, but not in the Merchants' Hall. Instead, because it was such an important occasion, it was held in the Usher Hall, which has a capacity of 2,200 people. The Princess and the Duke were seated at a table on the platform, between Colonel Drummond in his Master's high-backed chair and Sir Andrew Murray, Lord Provost of Edinburgh. Behind them, in the Organ Gallery, sat the combined choirs of the four Merchant Company schools, positioned there to sing a selection of songs.

The Secretary read out the formal Acts of Admission of the two new honorary members, and the Master made a speech praising the Royal Family's 'invaluable steadying force, whose influence for all that is good is incalculable'. The Company sincerely appreciated the honour conferred upon it, he said, and hoped that 'the ties that now bind us will grow in mutual trust and affection with the progress of the years'. So it has proved to be. Princess Elizabeth and the Duke then signed the Roll. Afterwards, they were entertained in the Merchants' Hall to lunch and an evening reception and dance. Commemorating the occasion, the Company's 12 Assistants added to its treasures a silver gilt cup, designed and made in Glasgow that same year by the goldsmith John Leslie Auld. It is 20.2 centimetres high, and is known as the Princess Elizabeth Cup.

Two years after that, the Very Reverend Dr Charles Warr, Minister of St Giles', was also made an honorary member, along with Lord Cooper, who was Lord President of the Court of Session, and Dr James Cameron Smail, the recently retired principal of Heriot-Watt College. As Dean of the Thistle and Chapel Royal, Dr Warr was to play an important part in the coronation celebrations in Scotland after Princess Elizabeth became Queen on the death of her father in 1952. The Merchant Company took particular pleasure in the celebrations because Her Majesty had agreed to become its Patron. The front of the Hanover Street Hall was decorated with teak

OPPOSITE.

Queen Elizabeth II by Sir William Hutchison (The Merchant Company; photograph ©John McKenzie Photography)

window boxes of flowers and hanging baskets at both porches, the railings were specially cleaned and a coronation souvenir in the form of an illustrated booklet was produced, entitled *The Historic Month of June 1953*. Two special copies bound in red morocco were delivered to Buckingham Palace for The Queen and the Duke of Edinburgh. The Master, Treasurer and Assistants gave a silver inkstand engraved with the Company's coat of arms and bearing the coronation hallmark. Made by Wilson and Sharp of Edinburgh, it cost £115 and was to be used by the new honorary members when they signed the Roll. Stanley Bennet, who became Master in 1953, later presented the Company with the Treasurer's Cup. Silver gilt and of German Renaissance design, it is inset with four seventeenth-century coins.

On 24 June 1953, The Queen would attend a special service in St Giles' to mark her first visit to Scotland since the coronation. The Honours of Scotland (the Scottish crown jewels) would be carried in procession before her and placed on the carved oak Communion Table. Thanks to an anonymous gift, Dr Warr had been able to have the Table cleverly extended in length by almost five inches so that there was room to display the crown, the sceptre and the sword of state. He also had plans to beautify the surrounding space. A late-nineteenth-century stone and marble arcade ran along the east wall behind the Table, but it had never been much liked, and Dr Warr was now eager to replace it with something more colourful. Several years earlier, Professor Sir A.E. Richardson of London University, asked to survey the Cathedral interior, had suggested taking out the arcade and installing a reredos, the sort of ornamental screen placed behind an altar in Roman Catholic and Anglican churches. This idea appealed to Dr Warr, and on 19 March 1953 he visited Master Dick Wood to suggest that The Merchant Company might like to make the gift of such a reredos to St Giles'. The

In Honour of T·R·H the Gift of the Ass.t Mast..

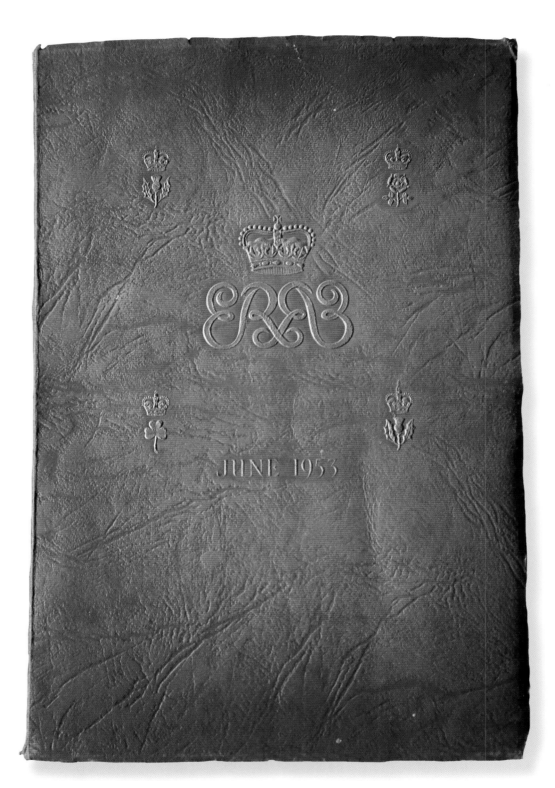

JUNE 1953

ABOVE.
Dr Charles Warr, Minister of St Giles' Cathedral, Chaplain to The Merchant Company and then Honorary Member, by Alfred Edward Borthwick (Courtesy of St Giles' Cathedral; photograph © Peter Backhouse)

OPPOSITE.
The Merchant Company Reredos in St Giles' Cathedral, watercolour by Sax Shaw (The Merchant Company; © John McKenzie Photography)

Company enthusiastically agreed, and far more than the requisite sum of £2,000 (almost £35,000 in present-day terms) was subscribed by the members. The surplus was used to set up a Master's Trust Fund for special Company expenditure.

Esmé Gordon, the Cathedral architect, designed a textile reredos 16 feet tall. It would be made of a rich golden brocade, and as part of its support it would have an oak post at either side, each with the carved figure of an archangel on top, representing St Michael and St Gabriel. The stone and marble arcade was removed, the wall was repaired and the reredos was installed just in time for the

Service of National Thanksgiving and Dedication. The televised service took place with great pomp and ceremony and the Master, Treasurer and Secretary of The Merchant Company sat proudly in their robes in a pew in the chancel, next to the city magistrates. The Cathedral was filled with flowers and the golden reredos shone brightly in the light. It had been much admired by The Queen when she had seen it the previous day at a rehearsal, and she had earlier written to thank The Merchant Company for their kindness. It was flanked by two copper plaques fixed to the wall behind it, one recording its gift by the Company and the other engraved with the Company Prayer. Above each plaque was a coat of arms, The Queen's on the left, The Merchant Company's on the right.

Sad to say, brocade is not as durable as stone and marble, and already by April 1955 Dr Warr was pointing out that the fabric was becoming tarnished. It was cleaned by the firm of Whytock and Reid, the leading cabinetmakers and furnishers in Edinburgh, but the problem persisted. The trouble was that the wall behind it had been repaired with cement, which draws the damp. Eventually, in April 1971, Dr Warr's successor, Dr Harry Whitley, who was by now The Merchant Company's Chaplain, had frequently criticised its dingy appearance, and he and the Kirk Session decided that it would have to be removed. Permission for any alterations at the Cathedral's east end would have to be sought from the Presbytery of Edinburgh and from the General Trustees of the Church of Scotland, but they knew that first of all they must discuss the matter with the generous donors, The Merchant Company. Master McIntosh Reid and his colleagues were very disappointed when the situation was explained to them at a series of meetings later in the year. They were particularly concerned about the feelings of their members. Many

ABOVE LEFT.
Bronze plaque
commemorating the gift
to St Giles' of the reredos
by The Merchant Company
(Courtesy of St Giles'
Cathedral; photograph
© Peter Backhouse)

ABOVE RIGHT.
The Merchant Company
coat of arms associated
with the St Giles' reredos
(Courtesy of St Giles'
Cathedral; photograph
© Peter Backhouse)

of those who had subscribed were still alive, and had expected the reredos to remain in place forever. At the same time, the St Giles' Session Clerk wrote to The Queen's Private Secretary explaining regretfully that the once-brilliant gold brocade could now only be described as drab, and hoping that Her Majesty would not be offended if it were removed.

The intention was to face the wall behind the Communion Table with stone. This would have the benefit of directing attention to the Table itself, 'which, of course', he said, 'is the main feature in a Presbyterian church'. The Queen's Private Secretary replied that Her Majesty had read the letter, recognised the need to remove the reredos and said that this would not, of course, detract in any way from her appreciation of The Merchant

Company's generosity. At a meeting on 13 December, the Master then expressed 'reasonable hope of minimal dissent by his members' if the fabric of the reredos were now to be cleaned and repaired by Whytock and Reid and displayed elsewhere. After much discussion, it was agreed that it should be used as a hanging behind the east processional door of the Thistle Antechapel, through which Her Majesty passed when going to services of the Order of the Thistle. The Church of Scotland authorities gave permission, and that was where the reredos textile was hung until it finally wore out. The wooden archangels were given to Esmé Gordon at his request, and the copper plaques were put in store in the Cathedral.

After the success of the 1953 Service of Thanksgiving and Dedication, it was decided

that in future The Merchant Company office-bearers should occupy a new pew of their own in the chancel of St Giles' on special occasions. It seats four. Above three of its stalls is carved the name of The Merchant Company, and each has on the back of the seat a roundel, two of them with the sea unicorn from the Company coat of arms and the other with a representation of the Stock of Broom. The fourth seat has no inscription or carving but was occupied by the Company Officer, holding their mace. When chairs replaced pews in the Cathedral in the late twentieth century, the pew was moved to the west end and, although it is no longer used, Company office-bearers continue to take part in, for example, the annual service for the Knights of the Thistle on the Sunday after St Andrew's Day.

Pleased to be part of these occasions, the Company were of a mind to strengthen further their long association with St Giles'. They resolved to make an annual donation of 10 guineas to the Cathedral and, no doubt at the suggestion of Dr Warr, they decided that they would like to have a special service to mark the appointment of a new Master. The first Kirking of the Master of The Merchant Company was held at noon on 20 January 1956, shortly after the election of Robert Wilson to that position, with the office-bearers attending in their robes, accompanied by the senior pupils from the schools. It was described afterwards as a beautiful occasion, and the kirking service now takes place every two years. In 1957 the Company appointed Dr Warr to be their Chaplain.

Meanwhile, they had also turned their

The Merchant Company pew in St Giles' Cathedral (Courtesy of St Giles' Cathedral; photograph © Peter Backhouse) attention to their own Hall. In the late 1940s, only vital maintenance work had been done, and by the early 1950s it was obvious that some interior improvements were needed. The vestibule was looking distinctly shabby, and so they had it panelled, with the gilded names of the Masters inscribed on the panelling. Master Dick Wood not only provided the panelling but presented a fine carved representation of the Company's coat of arms to be displayed there. The Queen's acceptance of the role of Patron gave further impetus to the improvements. The Board Room (Court Room) had not been decorated since 1932 and, when consulted in 1953, the distinguished architect Basil Spence advised that the walls should be covered with a suitable damask wallpaper. R. Muirhead and Sons duly sent in an estimate for £77 for doing the

papering and painting the ceiling. At the same time the Secretary's Room was redecorated for the first time since 1938, and it gained an interesting new feature. The former Merchants' Hall in Hunter Square was now occupied by the Royal Bank of Scotland, and in 1951 they kindly presented one of its wood and marble Adam fireplaces to the Company. Whytock and Reid adapted it in size to fit the Secretary's Room, and it was duly installed.

As to the hall, it had not been redecorated for the past 30 years, but in 1955 the Company commissioned a portrait of The Queen to be hung there. The artist was Sir William Hutchison, the distinguished President of the Royal Scottish Academy. The Queen gave him many sittings, inviting him to spend a week at Windsor Castle, where he would be able to observe her informally at mealtimes and relaxing in the evenings. He took photographs of his daughter, Elizabeth, wearing a long robe so that he could see how the folds would fall, and made many preliminary sketches. At the very first sitting, he painted The Queen's head on a small canvas so that he could refer to this direct and personal record as he went along. He later presented this sketch to the Scottish National Portrait Gallery. The full-length portrait, which cost 1,000 guineas, shows Her Majesty wearing the dark green velvet robe and gold collar of the Order of the Thistle, with a freely interpreted background of the interior of St Giles' Cathedral, where the Thistle Chapel is located.

Obviously this important acquisition must have suitable surroundings. Before it was placed in position, the hall was quickly redecorated and a musician's gallery, originally suggested by Old Master William Drummond, was constructed in the alcove above its entrance. Sir William Hutchison designed a special frame for his painting, with a scallop

at the top and carved swags at either side. He and William Kininmonth, the architect, were consulted about where exactly it should be displayed and at what height. With their advice, it was hung in a prominent position between the two windows, on the wall facing the doorway. It was unveiled on 18 October 1956 by Master Robert Wilson, in the presence of members of the Company and Lord Provost John Banks. The Company then planned a series of sherry parties to give members and their wives the opportunity of viewing the painting, and made arrangements for the public to be able to come and look at it.

There was quite a demand for colour prints of the portrait and the Company charged Scottish Television 25 guineas annually for using an image of it as a feature at the end of its daily programmes, in the way that the BBC did with Annigoni's famous portrait of The Queen. The following year the hall was further enhanced when its large central chandelier was dismantled and remodelled. Also, two important pieces of silver gilt were acquired for formal dinners held there. One is the oldest piece of plate in the Company's collection. It was presented by Master Robert Wilson in 1955 and had been chosen because it had been made in London in 1680–81, the latter being, of course, the year of the Company's charter. It is a porringer, 12 centimetres high, two-handled, and has a design of acanthus leaves, to which the Company added its own coat of arms. The second piece, designed by Alan Place and made in 1959 by Hamilton and Inches, took the form of a very elegant covered cup, 40.3 centimetres high, on a base of green onyx. It is engraved with four panels of the broom which forms the Company's emblem, and was designed to be used by the Treasurer to give the closing toast, 'The Stock of Broom', at formal Company dinners; and so it is known by that name. It was given to Master James Kennedy when he retired in 1959 and, following tradition, he presented it at once to the Company.

Throughout this period the stonework on the front of the Merchants' Hall was still giving trouble, and by 1963 almost £40,000 had been paid for repairs to it and for the insertion of four dormer windows in the top floor offices. Fortunately, the Company's finances were in a healthy state, not least because a change of investment policy had been successful. In 1949 Iver Salvesen had become Master. He had family connections with the Company, for his grandfather, Christian Salvesen, had been a member, and one of his uncles had been Lord Salvesen, the owner of Dean Park House. He himself had qualified as a chartered accountant and was by now running the family shipping and

OPPOSITE.
'The Stock of Broom' silver gilt cup (The Merchant Company; photograph © John McKenzie Photography)

BELOW.
Master Iver Salvesen (The Merchant Company Archive)

whaling business. During his term of office as Treasurer he had urged the Company to move some of its assets from property into stock exchange investments, since the latter involved no maintenance costs, as land did, and the dividends were more reliable. As a result, in March 1948 the Widows' Fund Trustees were agreeing to seek power to invest up to £50,000 in ordinary shares of companies such as J. & P. Coats, Distillers Company Limited, Dunlop Rubber, ICI, Scottish Brewers, Shell Transport and Trading, and F.W. Woolworth & Co.

The previous year the Company had begun to dispose of properties in Edinburgh, selling the Corporation 25 acres of land which they owned in the Pilton area of the city. This raised £15,000, and in January 1949 they sold the shop at 41 Shandwick Place. They had originally purchased it in 1900 for £10,000, and it now brought in £35,000, which in real terms was approximately twice the original value. The Widows' Fund owned a block of flats at 24 Morningside Road, and these were sold during the 1950s – apart from one, which was leased to a member of the teaching staff. The Widows' Fund gained £11,000 in 1953 from the sale of the shop at 46 South Bridge, Edinburgh. This did not mean that the Company had given up purchasing properties, however, and when 5 Church Lane Square (later named Gloucester Lane) came on the market the following year for £1,200, the Education Board snapped it up at once.

They also gained a new responsibility, however, in the form of the Fraser Homes for the elderly. Sir William Fraser, Deputy Keeper of the Records of Scotland, had made a small fortune by compiling histories of various aristocratic Scottish families based on their private archives, and from legal fees in peerage cases. He then used the proceeds to make shrewd investments. A personable man and very popular with the ladies, he never mar-

ried, but lived with his sister. When he died in 1898 at the age of 82, he left various handsome bequests. One was to establish the Sir William Fraser Chair of Scottish History and Palaeography at Edinburgh University and another was to found the Fraser Homes, attractive alms houses in Colinton for impoverished authors and artists. These consisted of 12 two-storey houses and a hall, run by the Sir William Fraser Trustees. In 1960, however, the Fraser Trustees gifted the homes to The Merchant Company. They were then administered by the Company's Fraser Homes Committee, consisting of the Fraser Trustees, along with representatives of the Endowments Trust. In future there would be a caretaker, who was paid £1 a week and lived free of charge in one of the houses, an almoner named Miss Cadger and a gardener. The Endowments Trust then embarked on a programme of modernising the Homes, spending over £20,000 installing kitchens and upstairs bathrooms, insulating ceilings and making sure that every living room had a sideboard. Some of the tenants did not want the sideboards and so, if they made an official

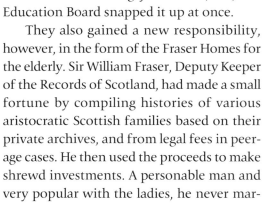

OPPOSITE.
One of a pair of silver gilt candelabra presented by Master Iver Salvesen (The Merchant Company; © John McKenzie Photography)

RIGHT.
Sir William Fraser by T. Faed (The Merchant Company)

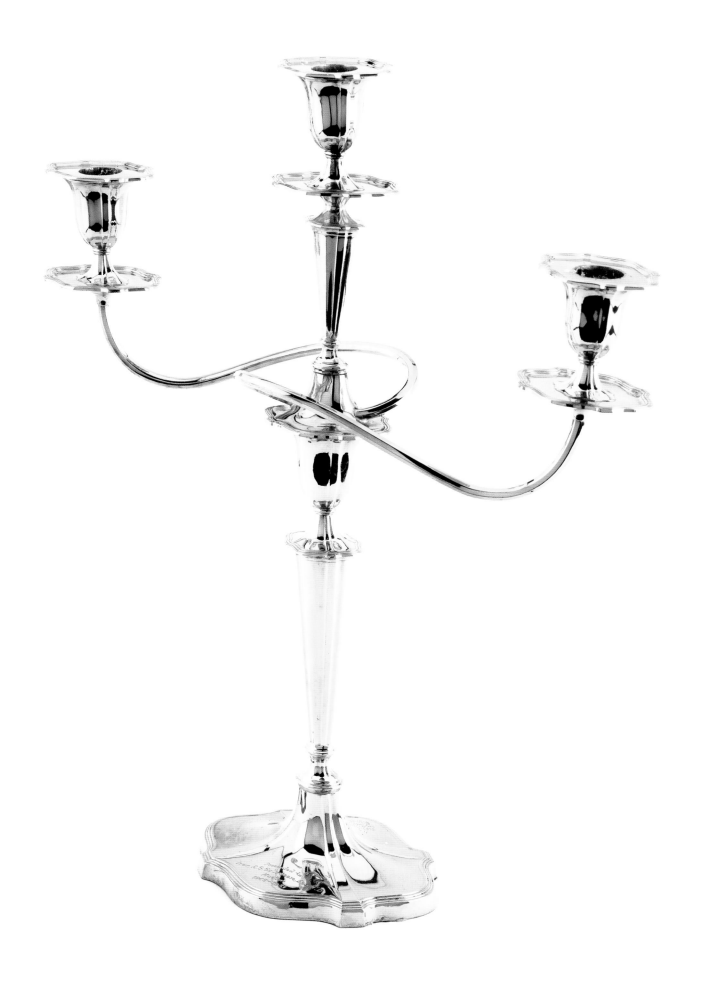

The Fraser Homes (© Steven Parry Donald Photography)

request, these could be put in store. A table and a dozen chairs placed in the communal hall were also regarded as superfluous and were taken away.

Throughout these years, of course, the Company continued to be preoccupied with the welfare of its schools. In June 1946, Edinburgh University indicated that it would like to extend its Medical School by acquiring the building occupied by George Watson's Ladies' College in George Square. The Company were reluctant to agree to this. They still planned to build a new George Watson's Ladies' College on the Liberton playing fields, but this could not happen for at least another 16 years, since the cost of Watson's new Boys' College would not be paid off until then. Nothing was done, but early in 1952 numbers 60 and 62 St Alban's Road came on the market, along with some vacant ground on the south side of the street. As these properties adjoined the preparatory department of George Watson's Ladies' College, the Company purchased them for almost £14,000.

That same year, the Town Clerk wrote to

the Company, announcing that the Town Council wished to acquire the land at Liberton, but the Education Board replied that they would only consider selling if an alternative site could be obtained on reasonable terms. Once more, nothing happened. The problem dragged on. By 1961 the City Development Plans showed a site for the new Ladies' College at Mortonhall, but the Company still preferred Liberton, not least because they owned 26.5 acres there, three acres more than the Mortonhall site. Meanwhile, Watson's Boys' College was taken up with a rather different accommodation consideration. More than a hundred boys were boarders, but there were no official school boarding houses. Instead, those boys who had to board were scattered about the town in private houses.

The Merchant Company was of the opinion that if they could offer official boarding houses, that would encourage even more parents to send their sons to Watson's, and so in September 1956 number 4 Gillsland Road was purchased and transformed into 'Bainfield',

the first official boarding house, named after the school's original playing field. It was run by one of the Mathematics teachers, W. Clark, under the supervision of a Board of Directors consisting of the Headmaster, three directors from The Merchant Company and three from the Watsonian Club's Council. Mrs Clark and a staff of three provided a home-like atmosphere. A second boarding house, 'Meadows House', was opened in 1958 at 7

Spylaw Road, and a third, 'Myreside House', in 1961 at 10 Ettrick Road.

As for the main Watson's Boys' College building, a government licence was required for any construction work during the immediate post-war years, and shortage of funds meant that there could be no ambitious extension plans. However, there were some welcome additions. On 13 November 1950, a fine new walnut-panelled library was opened by Old Master John S. Blair, who had given £3,500 towards its cost. An appeal for books was so successful that almost 6,800 volumes were donated, and in 1962 a classroom had to be adapted to become the additional Morrison Library. In 1956–7 the stand at the Myreside playing fields was infilled and used as an indoor cricket practice area, The Merchant Company paying half the estimated cost. An appeal raised the further sum necessary, one of the anonymous donors being Dr Jack Martin, a former pupil. He then went on to present an anonymous gift of no less than £35,000 for a new Music School. The architect Michael Laird was commissioned

ABOVE.
George Watson's Music School (Courtesy of George Watson's College)

LEFT.
Bainfield, George Watson's first boarding house (Courtesy of George Watson's College)

Presented
to
JOHN COWAN
BY THE
IRON & STEEL INSTITUTE
RECEPTION COMMITTEE
AS A MARK OF APPRECIATION OF
HIS SERVICES IN CONNECTION WITH
THE VISIT OF
AMERICAN ENGINEERS
1906

to design it. In the end, it cost over £48,630. It was triumphantly opened on 10 March 1964 by The Queen's cousin, Lord Harewood, who was at that time Director of the Edinburgh International Festival.

There were few changes at Daniel Stewart's building at this period. Although The Merchant Company had originally hoped to occupy Dean Park House at the end of the War, they instead offered to lease it to the Ministry of Defence in 1947, probably because they could not afford the cost of converting it at that point. Indeed, they did not take possession of it themselves until 1963. Meanwhile, the Mary Erskine School suffered a truly alarming disaster. The Queen Street building was in a sorry state, as a report by its Superintendent of Works in May 1950 made clear. The old north wing had been elaborately shored up and stiffened with cast-iron columns and steel beams, but in spite of these measures there had been a great deal of settlement, as was made obvious by cracks in the plasterwork, fractured lintels and unevenness in the floors. To add to the difficulties, there had been four outbreaks of dry rot in the previous three years; two of the classroom ceilings had recently been taken down because they were in a dangerous condition; and when a painter found a swinging ceiling in the staff dining room, the plasterer had to remove two tons of plaster, bringing down the lathing with it. Even the newer part of the school had a leaking roof and more plasterwork in a dangerous condition, with cracks in corridor ceilings. The Merchant Company Education Board, naturally alarmed at the possible danger, consulted the architectural firm of Reid and Forbes, who specialised in school work. They were told that, although it was safe to go on using the Queen Street building, that would only continue for a limited period and after essential repairs were undertaken.

Some necessary maintenance work was therefore carried out during the next few years, but on 20 January 1956, disaster struck. Mercifully, it was during the night that 13 of the ceilings collapsed, rendering the junior school classrooms unusable. As Muriel Jennings, the Headmistress, reported, 15 of the rooms in the old building had to be evacuated. The mess from the fallen plaster made the whole school dirty, and 9 of the 12 cleaners refused to go on working there and left. The janitor 'behaved splendidly but got very tired', and shortly afterwards the coal supply gave out and the boiler man, deciding that he was overworked, gave a week's notice. Fortunately, Muriel Jennings was equal to the situation. Tall, commanding and elegant, she had been Headmistress of an independent school in the south before taking up the appointment at Mary Erskine's in 1946 as its first English Headmistress.

Miss Jennings did not like The Merchant

OPPOSITE.
Silver gilt Monteith punch bowl presented in 1957 by A. Wallace Cowan (The Merchant Company; © John McKenzie Photography)

LEFT.
Muriel Jennings, Headmistress of Mary Erskine School (Courtesy of the Mary Erskine School)

Ravelston House, view from south (Courtesy of the Mary Erskine School)

house opposite, came on the market that spring. She convinced the Education Board that they must buy it. Three days after the purchase was completed at a cost of £4,500, the juniors moved in.

By the time that Muriel Jennings submitted her annual report in October 1956, she had been cheered by the news that some rebuilding in Queen Street would be possible, and she looked forward to the displaced pupils being able to move back there in due course. However, recent events had focused The Merchant Company's thoughts on a new site for Mary Erskine's: Ravelston House, on the west side of the city. This fine three-storey mansion had been built in about 1790 and stood in its own extensive grounds, with a walled garden, a seventeenth-century dovecot and a nineteenth-century stable and coach house. It was owned by Mrs James Clark, a philanthropic lady in her late eighties. She had originally intended leaving the house itself to the Church of Scotland, with the idea that it could become a home for the elderly. She meant to bequeath the grounds to the city, for they would make an attractive public park. However, for the past five years The Merchant Company had been negotiating with her agent in the hope that she would sell both house and grounds to them.

The Scottish Education Department was in favour of the idea, and the Town Council's Planning Sub-Committee decided that it would be willing to grant consent for the school to be built there. The estate was therefore surveyed in the autumn of 1956, but Mrs Clark could not make up her mind to abandon her original plans. However, early in 1960 she decided to put the house and estate up for sale, and her agent indicated that the price expected would be £125,000. The Merchant Company Education Board offered that amount, only to discover that they had been outbid by one of the Company's own

Company Secretary, H.M. Harvey-Jamieson. She resented being treated as an employee and having to seek his approval for her decisions, when she had directed policy and been responsible only to the governors at her previous school. However, in this emergency she and the Company Education Board worked hard together to deal with the crisis. A third of the school was sealed off behind cardboard partitions, and it was arranged to transfer the preparatory classes to the adjacent Kintore Rooms. Simpson House, further east in Queen Street at number 52, agreed to lease accommodation for two first junior year classes, and two other classes had to sit at their desks in corridors in the undamaged part of the school. Miss Jennings then came up with a more satisfactory solution. She lived in a flat in Ainslie Place, very near the school, and by a stroke of luck number 18, the

Ravelston House, view from north (Courtesy of the Mary Erskine School)

members, Thomas Boland, who owned a building firm and intended to develop the site. Aware of the Company's disappointment, however, he sold the mansion and part of the grounds to them for £110,700. That was a satisfactory outcome, but there then ensued further delays as a series of architectural plans was drawn up and rejected by the Company. William Kininmonth had been chosen to be the architect but, when he estimated the cost of converting the building at £1.25 million pounds, the Company said that this would be far too much. In 1962 they accepted a more modest plan, but then found that there was extensive dry rot in the house which would have to be treated. Lead was stripped off the roof and had to be replaced, and with all those complications it was 1964 before the Dean of Guild approved the final plans.

Muriel Jennings had many long and complicated discussions with the architect and The Merchant Company Secretary. She felt that the two men did not understand the practicalities of school design, but she exercised her famous technique for getting her own way. 'A woman must never score off men – never, never, never!' she would say, many years later, and instead she deployed all her well-practised charm and tact. In the end, she approved of the building, which she declared to be beautiful. The Earl of Mar and Kellie had become an honorary member of the Company in 1959, and the Countess laid the foundation stone of the new school in 1964. In March 1965 the Education Board agreed to sell the Queen Street building for £200,000 to City Wall Developments, who demolished it. A modern office block named Erskine House was erected in its place.

CHAPTER 7

A Royal Master, Pitsligo House and Tercentenary Celebrations: 1965–1981

On the afternoon of 11 November 1965, Prince Philip, Duke of Edinburgh was installed as Master of The Merchant Company. The ceremony took place at a special meeting in Parliament House's elegant Signet Library, once described by King George IV as 'the finest drawing room in Europe'. The Duke's predecessor, Master W. Fergus Harris, chairman of a large Leith timber merchant's business, presided. Immediately afterwards the Duke and the office-bearers walked in procession across Parliament Square to St Giles' Cathedral for his Kirking service, during which he read the New Testament Lesson from 1st Corinthians. In the evening he attended the Charter Dinner in the Merchants' Hall. Because of his many other commitments, he had accepted the position of Master for one year only instead of the usual two, and the Company had hastened to order a new robe for him from William Anderson & Sons, the Edinburgh tailors and outfitters.

The Duke was also the first to wear the new Master's Badge, which had been commissioned by John Mark Archer, the only son of Sir Gilbert Archer, in memory of his father. John, 'a great man of unfailing courtesy and kindness', was the Company Treasurer at that point. Now at the height of his career, he had

been awarded the CBE and, in the normal course of events, he would have succeeded as Master later that year. Sad to say, he had died on 28 August 1965 at the early age of 57, but the new Badge was ready. Designed by D. Shackman and Sons, Golden Square, the very prestigious London jewellers, and made by Hamilton & Inches, it takes the form of the Company's coat of arms. The famous sea unicorns are carved in nephrite, with sapphires for their eyes and diamonds set in the upper parts of their bodies. The globe is represented by a Scottish pearl and the thistles are made of emeralds and amethysts. The badge can be worn with the Master's Chain, or separately.

The Duke of Edinburgh brought all his customary energy and enthusiasm to his new role. He had warned the Company at the start that he could probably be only 'a paper Master' because of his 'circumstances'. Indeed, on the day of his installation, he had already toured a laboratory in East Kilbride, travelled by rail to Edinburgh and had lunch at the North British Hotel with the Edinburgh Chamber of Commerce. After the Merchant Company installation and kirking, he had visited the Christmas Market held in the Assembly Rooms in aid of the 50th Anniversary of

OPPOSITE.

Prince Philip, Duke of Edinburgh by Leonard Boden (The Merchant Company; © John McKenzie Photography)

the Scottish War Blinded, before attending the Merchant Company Dinner in the evening. Nevertheless, he managed to come to Merchant Company meetings or events on seven separate occasions during his year as Master, asked shrewd and searching questions and was particularly interested in the Merchant Company schools. He visited George Watson's Boys' College, and although he did not have time to see George Watson's Ladies' College too, Rosemary Colquhoun (later Woodroffe), Writer to the Signet, was at that time Head Girl and later recalled being presented to him at Colinton Road, along with her fellow prefects. Nor did his interest end with the conclusion of his year as Master. In 1973, for instance, while staying in the Palace of Holyroodhouse, he granted

an audience to the then Master, as he was anxious to be brought up to date with the Company's work.

In 1966 an award known as The Duke of Edinburgh's Trophy was initiated, to be given to the winning team competing in projects at the schools' increasingly popular outdoor centre at Ardtrostan, on Loch Earn. The following year, the Company mace was refurbished. For some time, members had noticed to their chagrin that its shaft was shorter than those of the maces of other organisations, and so Hamilton & Inches were asked to prepare a proposal to remodel it, not only lengthening it and generally improving its appearance, but incorporating the Duke of Edinburgh's coat of arms to commemorate his period of office. The Company likewise

ABOVE LEFT.
The Duke of Edinburgh cuts the cake at a Merchant Company event, watched by Master Ian Forbes (The Merchant Company Archive)

ABOVE RIGHT.
Prince Philip, Duke of Edinburgh by Leonard Boden (The Merchant Company; © John McKenzie Photography)

OPPOSITE.
The Merchant Company mace; detail, showing the coat of arms of the Duke of Edinburgh (The Merchant Company; © Steven Parry Donald Photography)

commissioned a portrait of the Duke, by Leonard Boden, the Glasgow artist said to be The Queen's favourite portrait painter. He had already painted the Duke on several occasions and, to help him along, the Company lent him the Duke's robe so that he could make preliminary sketches of it. The portrait cost £1,298, was unveiled on 9 February 1967 and shows the Duke seated in the Master's high-backed chair in his robes and chain, the badge of office suspended at his neck and the mace partially visible on a table beside him.

The Company's connection with the Royal Family was further strengthened when Queen Elizabeth The Queen Mother was installed as an honorary member on 18 Octo-ber 1967, visiting the Merchants' Hall in 'a turquoise blue silk coat and dress with matching feather hat', as the *Scottish Daily Express* reported. Master Ian Forbes welcomed Her Majesty. He was Director of Stewart & Company, Seedsmen Limited and a former President of the Royal Caledonian Horticultural Society. Aware that she was a keen gardener, he had prepared an appropriately gallant compliment, telling her that she was like '*tropaeolum speciosum*, sometimes known as the Highland Flame flower – which, having roots in a cool place toward the north, produces a glorious flourish on a southern aspect'. The Queen Mother, no doubt amused, responded graciously.

Ten years later, The Queen's Silver Jubilee

Queen Elizabeth The Queen Mother greeted at the Merchant Company Hall by Treasurer W.G. Macmillan, with Master Ian Forbes looking on, 1967 (The Merchant Company Archive)

of 1977 was a major national event, with a splendid dinner in the Merchants' Hall. Every pupil in the Company schools was given the specially minted commemorative coin, a Jubilee crown piece, and Her Majesty's portrait by Sir William Hutchison was lent to the Scottish National Portrait Gallery to be the centrepiece in their celebratory display. Two years after that, Charles, Prince of Wales accepted an invitation to become an honorary member of the Company. When he married Lady Diana Spencer in 1981, the Company sent as a wedding gift 12 crystal wine glasses engraved with its crest. On the subject of honorary members, the Company

had by then lost several, with the deaths of the Very Reverend Dr Charles Warr, Dr Smail and Lord Bilsland of Kinrara, but they had gained Lord Erskine of Rerrick in 1970 (already an ordinary member), Lord Home (Sir Alec Douglas-Home) in 1972, and the Earl of Elgin and Kincardine and Lord Clydesmuir, both in 1973. Dr Harry Whitley had retired as the Company's Chaplain that year because of ill-health and was replaced by the Very Reverend Ronald Selby Wright, Minister of the Canongate Kirk and a well-known figure in Edinburgh and beyond, not least because of his popular broadcasts as Radio Padre during the war.

The ordinary membership of the Company was flourishing too, and reached a record total of 791 members in 1974. As Old Master William Grierson Macmillan had remarked a few years earlier, a high membership was not an important objective in itself, but a token of the Company's stature and significance in the city. Indeed, although he did not say so, this could also be seen reflected in the number of invitations he had received as Master to the dinners of other Scottish organisations and the impressive English livery companies. A director of Melrose's tea firm, he was the grandson of Master John Macmillan, who had died so suddenly in 1901.

His father, the original Master Macmillan's fourth son, had also been a tea merchant and one of the Company's Assistants. This sort of dynasty of members was far from being unusual. As well as the Macmillans, Salvesens and Archers, there were successive Crabbies (Leith wine and spirits merchants), Dowells (auctioneers), Thins (booksellers), Yerburys (photographers) and others. This was in part because it was traditional for sons to join their fathers in the family business in those days, and in part because they were encouraged to become Company members because of the contacts and prestige that it brought them.

LEFT.
Andrew, 11th Earl of Elgin and 15th Earl of Kincardine, Honorary Member of The Merchant Company (Charlestown Lime Heritage Trust; © RCAHMS Licensor www.rcahms.gov.uk)

RIGHT.
The Very Reverend Ronald Selby Wright, Chaplain to The Merchant Company (Scottish National Portrait Gallery)

ABOVE.
Master William Grierson
Macmillan, grandson of
Master John Macmillan
(The Merchant Company
Archive)

OPPOSITE.
The Master's Lady's gold
brooch, in the shape of the
Company mace (© Steven
Parry Donald Photography)

£320. Meanwhile, Old Master Hugh Rose, the Cambridge-educated Director of the family firm of Craig and Rose, paint manufacturers and decorators, gave a brooch in the form of the Stock of Broom for successive Treasurers' Ladies to wear on official occasions. As it had become a tradition for a Master to give back to the Company his retirement gift, he also presented them with the silver gilt lectern which he had been given when he retired. In a similar manner, when the previous Old Master W.S. McIntosh Reid accepted four crystal decanters with engraved silver gilt wine labels and coasters in 1973, he immediately passed them back to the Company.

Shortly after this time, a new connection was made with the Guildry of Edinburgh. As we have seen, the medieval Merchant Guild had lost much of its influence in the sixteenth century and its powers of regulating trade had vanished too. However, when the Merchant Company was chartered in 1681, the Merchant Guild continued to exist as a separate institution known as the Guildry of Edinburgh, responsible for giving planning permission for all building activities in the city. After the Local Government (Scotland) Act 1973, the creation of Edinburgh District Council two years later meant that the Guildry would no longer have administrative facilities and might even lose the use of the Dean of Guild Court Room in the City Chambers. That did not in fact happen, but some months earlier Edinburgh's Lord Dean of Guild, Ian Mackenzie, wrote to Master Hugh McMaster about the problems facing the Guildry, most of whose members were also members of the Merchant Company. The Master was sympathetic and had already suggested that the secretarial duties of the Guildry could be undertaken by the Merchant Company staff. The relationship became closer still when it was subsequently agreed that in future the Guildry would elect

Members with a family connection to the Company naturally felt a particularly strong identification with it. After his term of office, Master W. Grierson Macmillan presented a gold brooch in the shape of the Company mace, to be worn in future by Masters' Ladies; and John M. Archer's son Gilbert continued his family's generosity with the gift in 1974 of a special chair for the Treasurer, in memory of his father. The Company then felt that there ought to be a matching chair for the Secretary, and purchased one at a cost of

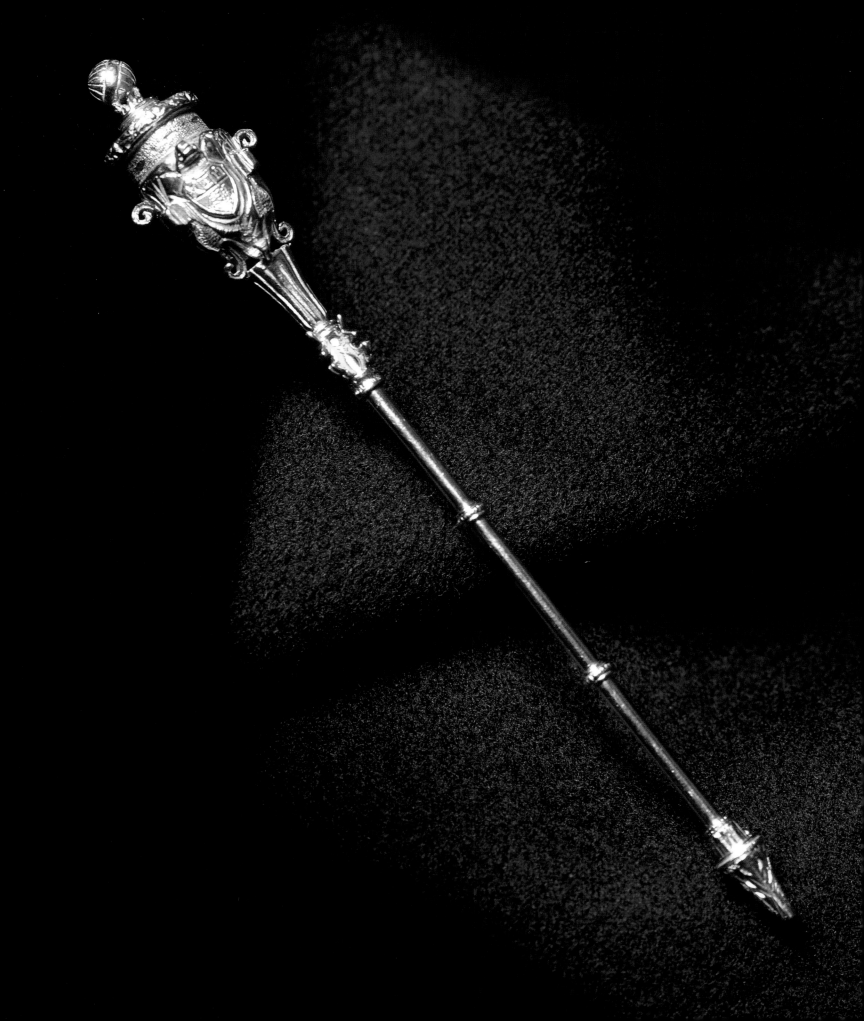

as Lord Dean of Guild the most recent Old Master of the Company. Since then, the Lord Dean of Guild has taken part in the ceremonial occasions of the Company, resplendent in his ermine-trimmed scarlet robe.

There were other developments too, for in 1968, the Company office-bearers had been taken with the idea of transforming the Merchants' Hall into what they termed 'a Mercantile Centre'. They were well aware that their Hall was not fully occupied. Certainly all the schools' administration was run from there, but some of the largest rooms were rarely used and that was uneconomic. As a result, various internal changes took place. The British Linen Bank was persuaded to move from number 20 to the ground floor of number 24, which meant that the Company could lease number 20 to the Edinburgh Chamber of Commerce instead. At the end of April 1970 the Chamber moved in and shared the Company's secretarial and accounting services. Likewise Polecon Company Limited, an economic research company, took a suite of rooms on the second floor of number 22. An executive conference suite had been established at number 18, and in 1973 a top-floor room there was leased, appropriately, to the Scottish representative of the *Financial Times*. AVCO Financial Services Ltd took over the British Linen Bank's lease in May 1976 'at a considerably higher rate'. The Carnegie Trust was still a tenant, and both the Board Room (Court Room) and the executive conference suite were by then much in demand as accommodation for meetings held by outside organisations. All these arrangements were very beneficial financially to the Company and convenient both for themselves and for the various tenants, as well as emphasising their shared interests.

Meanwhile, care for the elderly was expanding significantly. The Widows' Fund

was in a very satisfactory state, and in 1972 it stood at around £1.25 million, with the 200 or so beneficiaries each receiving £272 a year. Apart from looking after the widows of their own members, the Company also had to make sure that their Endowments Trust investments were doing well. The Drumsheugh Place properties, for instance, brought in a good annual revenue and so, when the Endowments Trust received an offer for one of the flats in 1965, they promptly refused it. Three years later, however, they did sell two of the flats, receiving £120,000 for each, and

ABOVE.
Master Hugh Rose (The Merchant Company Archive)

OPPOSITE.
Treasurer's Lady's brooch, in the shape of the stock of broom (© Steven Parry Donald Photography)

Pitsligo House, formerly
Newbattle House (The
Merchant Company Archive)

in 1970 they were seriously considering dis-
posing of two more. These had lain vacant
for quite some time and they were now in a
very dilapidated state. In fact, one of them
had actually been vandalised, and so the
Company Secretary advised the Endowments
Trust to sell them as soon as possible. This
they did, and improved the others by
rewiring them. In 1975 the Endowments Trust
was able to rent three of the flats to Edinburgh University on a full repairing and
insuring lease.

The Endowments Trust routinely used
some of its income to modernise its existing
homes for the elderly, but in 1966 there was
a highly important development when the
Company unexpectedly acquired Newbattle
House, a home for elderly ladies. This had
been founded by Dr Jack Martin, the generous benefactor of George Watson's College.
A son of John G. Martin, who owned a well-
known bakery firm in Edinburgh, Dr Martin
was born in 1904 and had been a pupil at
George Watson's. He first of all took the new
degree of Bachelor of Commerce at Edin-

burgh University before spending ten years
in the family firm. However, he had always
longed to be a doctor, and in 1937 his father
agreed that he should leave the bakery business and return to Edinburgh University to
study medicine. In due course he graduated
with an MB, ChB, and for a short time he was
in general practice. As a result of his experi-
ences he became very much aware of the
need for homes for the elderly, and so he
bought a large house at the corner of Newbattle Terrace and Pitsligo Road in Morningside. Very soon, he was looking after about a
dozen elderly ladies in Newbattle House for
a weekly charge of three guineas each. He
then purchased the house next door in Newbattle Terrace, adding a connecting building
which served as the dining room. This
allowed him to care for still more elderly
ladies, all of whom were devoted to him.

Anxious to secure the home's future, he
decided that he could best achieve that by
passing it on to the Merchant Company,
transferring not only the building itself with
its furnishings and fittings but £20,000

(worth more than ten times that amount in 2005) in investments and cash. The Company were happy to accept this new responsibility, and Dr Martin continued to visit his old and new friends in the house at least twice a week. Devoted to medicine and music, and an enthusiastic cricketer and golfer, he would eventually become the oldest member of Mortonhall Golf Club. After a stroke in 1986, he spent his remaining years in a nursing home, where he died in 1991 after his long life of service. More than 20 years later, Old Master Brian Adair would remember him affectionately as 'the kindest of men, modest, unassuming, a friend to everyone who required help'.

In February 1967, the Endowments Trust set up a Newbattle Committee to deal with this important acquisition, raising the weekly charge to residents to £8 and providing for their continued welfare, comfort, maintenance and support, as well as making available at a low cost any necessary care and nursing. By end of the year the Trust was planning not only to modernise the existing accommodation but to add an extension with 18 bedrooms, a small sick bay, improved kitchen premises and a self-contained flat for the matron. This doubled the amount of accommodation at a cost of £117,000, providing, in all, rooms for 40 elderly residents. While the work was going on the occupants were moved out to stay in a hotel in North Berwick, which they enjoyed greatly. The fine new extension was completed in September 1970 and the name of the home was then changed to Pitsligo House, after the street in which it was situated. This would avoid confusion with another Newbattle House, a former manse in Midlothian.

The residents pronounced themselves to be very happy with all the improvements and when Mrs Butter, the efficient matron, retired in 1973 she was replaced by Miss

A resident and Thora Bissett, who succeeded Miss Cadger as Matron, at the doorway of Pitsligo House (The Merchant Company Archive)

Cadger, who would combine her role with her existing position as the Endowments Trust almoner. A few years later, the Endowments Trust decided that it must install a geriatric unit at Pitsligo House. The cost was estimated at £51,000 and so it was decided to sell the four flats at Gilmore Place to finance it. The total sum realised from the flats was £60,907, and a further £2,000 was raised by selling part of the rear garden there to K&I Coachworks. The sales were completed in 1979, the same year in which the geriatric unit opened, providing an extra five rooms for frail residents.

The Company's work with the elderly was by now very well known, and in 1969, Captain Harold K. Salvesen had decided to give them Whitehouse Park, over seven and a half acres of land adjoining his house in Cramond. The Captain, who had significantly developed his family firm's whaling activities, wished the proceeds from his gift to be used for the benefit of elderly people who would be known as Christian Salvesen Pensioners, in memory of his grandfather.

Unfortunately, Captain Salvesen died on 1 February 1970, within a year of making the gift, which meant that Estate Duty had to be paid at 80%. Plans for the pensioners were abandoned, but the proceeds from the sale nevertheless added a substantial amount to the funds of the Endowments Trust. Also in 1970, the Trust was discussing the possibility of building flats for the elderly on Westhall Tennis Courts, which were owned by the Company's Education Board; but this idea could not be followed up because the Education Board had something else in mind, and in 1974 sold Westhall to the Heritable Development Consultancy Limited for £72,000.

Endowments owned for the benefit of the schools also had to be carefully managed, and Peterhead continued to be an important source of revenue for Mary Erskine's. Relationships with both the town and the tenants were, as always, harmonious, and in 1969 the Education Board agreed to transfer Peterhead Cemetery to the town. As well as relieving the Board of the burden of maintenance, this was what the townspeople wished. When in 1971, A.E.M. Taylor completed 45 years as the Company's Peterhead Estate Officer, Master McIntosh Reid along with the Treasurer and the Secretary, visiting Peterhead for one of their regular inspections, presented him with a copy of Alexander Heron's Company history, in recognition of his long service. They later disposed of just under two and a quarter acres at Little Grange to Peterhead Town Council.

In 1973 the Trustees of the Widows' Fund decided that it would be wise for them to include some property in their holdings, and so the Education Board obligingly sold them the farms at Blackhills and East Barnyards, Peterhead, for £24,000 and £75,000 respectively. The Widows' Fund then went on to sell the double cottage at Middle Barnyards to the sitting tenant, at his request, and with the help of grants, they made major improvements at Blackhills Farm. On the subject of sales, the Education Board disposed of various other properties at that time. All three boarding houses for George Watson's boys were put on the market, since a new boarding house was to be built in the school grounds. The sale of Bainfield House, Meadows House and Myreside House brought in over £470,000. The outdoor centre at Ardtrostan was sold too, in 1981, for £60,000.

Dedicated to their charitable activities and anxious to raise their profile, the Merchant Company were delighted when Edinburgh District Council agreed to put on a major exhibition in the winter of 1978–9 entitled 'The Stock of Broom: An Exhibition of the Treasures of Edinburgh Merchant Company'. It would be held in the Canongate Tolbooth in the Royal Mile. The Queen graciously agreed to be Patron of the exhibition, and sent a letter to Master Kenneth Ryden thanking him for the loyal greetings dispatched to her on the eve of its opening on 9 November 1978. The exhibition was in three main sections. The first surveyed the history of the Company, beginning with a display of precious documents including the 1681 Charter with the great seal of Charles II attached to it and the first Roll Book of members' signatures, begun that same year.

William Hole's imaginary painting of the first meeting of the Company (usually in the Court Room) was hung on the wall in that section, and other items included the mace and the Master's robe and badge. The second section comprised a glittering array of the Company's silver gilt plate including, of course, the famous ship centrepiece, the Stock of Broom cup and the Princess Elizabeth cup. The third and final section was hung with portraits of important figures such as George Watson and Daniel Stewart, and in the showcases there were documents and plans of the various endowed hospitals. The exhibition, accompanied by an attractively illustrated catalogue written by Maurice Berrill, the Assistant Secretary, ran until 27 January 1979 and evoked much interest.

That same year a dinner to celebrate the Merchants' Hall's 100 years in Hanover Street was held after improvements there costing £20,000. A whole series of exciting events was on the horizon, for 1981 would see the tercentenary of the 1681 Royal Charter. As early as 1976 the Master's Court had set up a working party to plan the celebrations. Master Raoul Boothman's Kirking service was postponed for several months until 1981, the next Charter Dinner would also be held in 1981 and two years beforehand Films of Scotland began planning a film to mark the occasion. Moreover, The Queen and the Duke of Edinburgh agreed to visit the Merchants' Hall during the tercentenary year. The Kirking service was duly held on 12 February 1981 and the film *The Stock of Broom* was shown in Morningside's Dominion Cinema on 3 May. It began with a sequence taken when the Chaplain, the Very Reverend Ronald Selby Wright, said the Merchants' Prayer before the admission of two new members; this was followed by scenes of pupils in the Company schools working in classrooms and enjoying the fine recreational facilities. The National Library of Scotland preserved a copy of the film, which was later digitised and made available on their website.

Continuing the celebrations, an Endowments Trust Garden Party was held at Pitsligo House on 22 May and the Merchant Company schools celebrated with a Festival Week in late June. The high point came on 7 July, when The Queen and the Duke of Edinburgh arrived as promised at the Tercentenary Reception held in the Merchants' Hall

An Exhibition of the Treasures of the Edinburgh Merchant Company

and signed their names not only on a portrait photograph of themselves but on the first page of a specially commissioned Distinguished Visitors' Book, which the Old Masters had presented to the Company. The Queen was given a fine new brooch in the form of the Company coat of arms, and Maurice Berrill later recalled how touched those present were when she immediately unpinned the brooch she was wearing and

The Stock of Broom exhibition catalogue, by Maurice Berrill, 1978 (Photograph of cover © Steven Parry Donald Photography)

RIGHT.
The Queen signing the portrait photograph of herself and the Duke of Edinburgh, 1981 (The Merchant Company Archive)

OPPOSITE.
The Queen at the Tercentenary Reception in the Merchant Company Hall, 1981 (The Merchant Company Archive)

put it on instead. Coincidentally, the Royal College of Physicians were celebrating their own tercentenary that year, and so the two organisations held receptions for each other's members.

Gifts flowed in too. Peterhead Harbour Trustees gave a silver gilt coffee service with tray, Master Boothman gave back a pair of silver gilt bowls which he had received from the Company and the Assistants presented a mahogany side table with a suitable inscription. The Scottish Stock Exchange gave a handsome three-pedestal luncheon table with two carver chairs and 36 upright chairs, and the Edinburgh Stock Exchange added another table with 24 matching chairs. Sir Alistair Blair presented a history of the law firm, Messrs Davidson and Sime. Finally, to help the celebrations along, the Company decided to purchase some Tercentenary Claret of Saint-Emilion to sell to members 'at the appropriate price'. This proved to be such a success that further bottles had to be hastily ordered to satisfy the demand.

CHAPTER 8

Saving the Schools:
1965–1981

The successes and celebrations of the 1960s and 70s were more than a little over-shadowed for The Merchant Company by a growing educational crisis which came to threaten the very existence of its schools. Children in state schools sat an examination at the age of 11 to determine which school they should attend next. In Scotland, the 30% who were judged to be more academic went on to a high school while the majority attended what was known as a junior secondary. The high school pupils were expected to spend five or six years there, after which they sat their Higher Examinations; and then fewer than 5% of them went on to study at a university. The junior secondary majority left at the age of 15, without any qualification. The Scottish Education Department decided in the early 1960s that they must introduce a new O grade certificate at the end of the fourth year so that those leaving at 15 could have a more structured education and feel more motivated as a result. The first of these certificates were awarded in 1962.

As leaders in secondary education, The Merchant Company were very interested in this development. Roger Young, Headmaster of Watson's Boys' College since 1959, was particularly involved, and would eventually be knighted as one of the leading educationists in Britain. He approved of the O level certificate, but was concerned that all pupils had to sit it, knowing as he did that it was too demanding for some of the candidates. Informed of his views in two lengthy papers, The Merchant Company appointed him to chair a Working Party for the Less Academic Boy. It reported in the summer of 1965 and, as a result, a new course was established for those boys who would sit only three or four O levels, with the emphasis being on a wide range of activities aimed at preparing them for life after school.

So far, so good; but in 1964 Labour had won the General Election, with Harold Wilson as Prime Minister, and the new Government was determined to do away with the two-tier system of education throughout Britain. In England, the grammar schools would be abolished. The Scottish Education Department issued a circular stating that all Scotland's state secondary schools would now become comprehensive, with no selection process at the end of primary school. The Merchant Company were not unduly concerned at first, for they already operated an all-through policy, providing education for children from the nursery stage until they

141

Roger Young, Headmaster of George Watson's Boys' College (Courtesy of George Watson's College)

left school. Moreover, they were aware that they had a broader academic and social mix than was the case in many of the English grammar schools. At the same time, they were convinced that 'able children can achieve as high academic standards at Merchant Company schools as at any other schools'. In responding to the Scottish Education Department circular, they emphasised that they had always been at the forefront of educational thought in Scotland and were determined to lead and not to follow in this area. That said, they stressed that their first concern was for the welfare of the pupils in their schools.

Even so, The Merchant Company knew that they were in a potentially vulnerable position, for it was widely rumoured that the Government would not only merge junior secondaries with high schools but was deter-

mined to abolish fee-paying schools altogether. The Company therefore decided to set up a working party to consider what might lie ahead. It consisted of the Company Secretary, H.M. Harvey-Jamieson (the old adversary of Muriel Jennings) and the head teachers of the four schools. Roger Young of George Watson's Boys' College was there, and Hilda Fleming, a tall and, some thought, rather intimidating Yorkshirewoman with a degree in physics, who was now in charge at George Watson's Ladies' College. Jean Thow had succeeded Muriel Jennings at Mary Erskine's when the school moved to Ravelston. A Scot and a Modern Languages graduate, she was gentle, courteous and determined. Bertram T. Bellis, a mathematician particularly interested in the new science of computing, was Headmaster of Daniel Stewart's.

Pleased with the all-through nature of

their schools, the Working Party nevertheless recommended that this aspect should, if possible, be strengthened to deflect any forthcoming criticism, and turned their attention to the vitally important financial implications of the Government's intended policies. Fee-paying schools in Edinburgh were widely criticised for creaming off the best pupils. There were far more fee-paying schools in the capital than elsewhere in Scotland, and they fell into three categories. Some local authority schools were fee-paying, as of course were the totally independent schools. The Merchant Company schools belonged to a third group of 29 Scottish schools which charged fees but also received a government grant. In Edinburgh, George Heriot's, Melville College, John Watson's and St Mary's Cathedral Choir School also came into this category.

The Merchant Company relied upon their government grant to pay for up to 60% of their expenditure. The rest came from the fees they charged and from their investments. The government grant was what allowed them to keep fees at about half the economic cost and give financial assistance to foundationers whose families could not afford to pay the full amount. The Working Party thought that they could perhaps render their schools more acceptable to the Government by attracting more pupils who could not afford the fees. They were even prepared to welcome a scheme whereby fees were graded according to the ability to pay, so that the government grant would not be applied to all fees equally. Conscious that there was always a great demand for places from parents who had themselves been educated at Merchant Company schools, the Working

Party suggested that this impression of exclusivity could be reduced if 50% of places were awarded to applicants with no previous connection with the schools.

The question of co-educational schooling had also arisen, because that was the system favoured by the Government. How could The Merchant Company satisfy this, when they had two separate schools for boys and two for girls? There was, they felt, room for both systems, but they were willing to concede rather tentatively that there could be a certain amount of cooperation between the boys' schools and girls' schools, depending, of course, upon the reaction of the parents to such a proposal. For instance, a music school could be built at Ravelston for use by both Mary Erskine's and Daniel Stewart's. If that was not deemed to be enough, they had an even more radical proposal. George Watson's Ladies' College was going to have to be rebuilt in the near future, because of Edinburgh University's longstanding desire to acquire its George Square site. The University Athletic Ground at Craiglockhart had recently been re-zoned by the City as a site for the Ladies' College. It was adjacent to Watson's Boys' College, and so the two schools could be merged into one at Colinton Road.

A new building would house co-educational primary classes 1 to 5, while 6 and 7 would stay in the existing Boys' College preparatory block and the secondary classes would be in the main building. Hilda Fleming was strongly in favour of this solution, and Roger Young was enthusiastic too. If implemented, the plan would mean that The Merchant Company could offer parents a choice of single-sex education at Mary Erskine's and Daniel Stewart's or co-education at Watson's, and this might satisfy the Scottish Education Department. These hopeful proposals were contained in the Working Party Report when it was published in 1967, but there was little that it could suggest with regard to finance. Certainly, because Mary Erskine's was now at Ravelston, the Board were able to put on the market 18 Ainslie Place, which they had hastily purchased at the time of the Queen Street building problems. Even so, the amount that would bring in would be a drop in the ocean compared with the sum required, and the threat to the grant-aided schools loomed ever larger.

The following year, the recently established Public Schools' Commission issued its first report. It dealt mainly with English boarding schools, but it then proceeded to its next investigation, which was to include the Scottish grant-aided schools. It was reassuring that Roger Young was a member of the Commission and Vice Chairman of the Scottish Sub-Committee, but The Merchant Company remained apprehensive about the results, and with good reason. The Government proceeded to freeze their grant. In 1969 it was reduced, future prospects looked very gloomy indeed, and even after the election of a Conservative Government led by Edward Heath that year, The Merchant Company remained wary. Certainly the Scottish Education Department told them that the Secretary of State for Scotland had assured him that the new Government would be 'well-disposed' to grant-aided schools, but who knew what would really happen?

The Merchant Company decided that it would be prudent to set up three new groups to keep a close watch on the situation. The Research Group, consisting of the four head teachers, would examine in detail matters referred to it. A South Side Sub-Committee, chaired by Roger Young, would consider the amalgamation of Watson's Boys' and Ladies' Colleges, and a North Side Sub-Committee, chaired by Bertram T. Bellis, would re-examine the 1967 Working Party Report in so far as it affected Mary Erskine's and Daniel Stewart's. Meantime, in 1970, the Company happily celebrated the centenary of the 1870 reorganisation of their schools with a sumptuous dinner held at Hanover Street.

After this pleasant interlude, on 26 March 1971 Teddy Taylor, Under-Secretary of State for Health and Education, invited the Scottish grant-aided secondary schools to set up a special committee which would submit proposals for the future level, use and conditions of the grant they needed. There would be five sub-committees for the different geographical areas of Scotland and an overarching Central Committee for the Grant-Aided Schools in Scotland, with Master McIntosh Reid of The Merchant Company as its chairman. He could see that the matter would have to be handled very carefully, in a way that would antagonise neither the Government, the public nor indeed any of the other grant-aided schools themselves. That summer the grant regulations were debated in Parliament and the attitude of the Labour opposition was made clear when Norman Buchan MP, Shadow Under-Secretary of State for Health and Education in Scotland, declared, 'We now know what we should be doing with the grant-aided schools. We should be moving them into the general public sector.' This had been the conclusion of the Public Schools Commission's Second Report.

After even more careful thought and a series of meetings, Master McIntosh Reid completed his Central Committee's Report, asking for government funding to cover 50% of the grant-aided schools' expenditure. The Report was passed to the Secretary of State for Scotland in January 1972. However, the final amount of the grant had still not been fixed when Master McIntosh Reid retired that autumn, although the sum was now expected to provide only about 40% of the

Teddy Taylor, MP (© Euro Realist Newsletter, licensed under CC by SA 2.0)

schools' running costs. The following February a new crisis erupted, which made matters much worse. It was announced by the Scottish Education Department that every Scottish teacher would receive a flat rate increase in salary of £141 from 1 April. How were The Merchant Company going to afford this? They still did not know the level of government grant they could expect for 1973–4. They immediately requested a meeting with the Scottish Education Department and, as Chairman of the Central Committee, Old Master McIntosh Reid wrote on 22 February 1973 to Hector Monro, Parliamentary Under-Secretary of State for Health and Education, urging him to intervene personally on behalf of such schools. It was extremely urgent that they should be told the level of that year's grant as soon as possible, he said, and he pointed out that it was now more than a year since his Central Committee had submitted its report as requested.

A meeting with Scottish Education Department officials eventually took place on 5 March 1973, but the results were extremely disappointing and Master McIntosh Reid felt impelled to write to Hector Monro once again that day. 'We were promised nothing,' he complained. Indeed, it had even been suggested that they should dip into

Master McIntosh Reid (The
Merchant Company Archive)

their capital reserves – which was simply not possible. A fee increase would be needed to pay the teachers at their new salary scale, and it would be more than most parents could afford. The response to his protest would, he said, be seen as 'the acid test of the Government's statement of March 1971 that "the schools had the real goodwill of the Government"'. Meanwhile, The Merchant Company had no alternative but to raise its school fees that spring, for the first time in two years.

Some progress was eventually made by 8 November 1973 after a meeting with Hector Monro himself, and as a result, a small working party of Scottish Education Department officials and members of the Central Committee for Grant-Aided Schools in Scotland

was set up to consider proposals for the future basis of the grant. However, anxieties increased again when, at the next General Election on 28 February 1974, Labour came to power once more. Actually, there was a hung parliament, but Harold Wilson formed a minority government, and when he called another election on 10 October 1974 he obtained a majority of three. His government proceeded to freeze the schools' grant again and announced that they would now develop fully their comprehensive system of education, phasing out the grant-aided schools and offering to integrate them into the state system. At the same time, the Houghton Report was published, recommending a major retrospective increase in teachers' salaries. As a result of all this, some Edinburgh grant-aided schools were being forced to close down altogether, unable to keep going because of the financial difficulties, while there was talk of others perhaps becoming Merchant Company schools.

George Heriot's considered this way forward but decided against it and became fully independent. However, both Melville College and John Watson's were interested.

Melville College building, 2015, in Melville Street, now mainly offices (© Ian Watson)

Aerial view of George Watson's College (Courtesy of George Watson's College)

Melville College had been founded in 1832 by the Reverend Robert Cunningham as The Edinburgh Institution for Languages and Mathematics. After it moved to Melville Street it was re-named. In 1972 a joint working party with The Merchant Company had been set up to discuss the proposal that it should integrate with Daniel Stewart's, which was not far away. The working party quickly decided that the arguments in favour of a merger were overwhelming. This would create a single all-through primary and secondary school. The Limited Company known as 'Melville College' was therefore wound up on 30 September 1972, its net assets were transferred to The Merchant Company Education Board and the amalgamation was completed by 8 November 1973, with new blazers incorporating the colours of both schools and a new badge combining their armorial bearings.

Meanwhile, The Merchant Company had been proceeding with its plans to merge the two George Watson's Colleges. When this had first been suggested by the Education Board Working Party in 1967, the idea had not been rejected, and indeed it seems to have received a cautious welcome. Nothing happened at once, but the Board had decided in 1971 that they would proceed with the scheme. The Scottish Education Department had approved the plan, the George Square premises were sold to the University for £485,000, the Athletic Ground was purchased from the University at a cost of £100,000 and the first joint school assembly was held on 1 October 1974. In spite of the uncertain financial future, a good deal of building would have to take place at Colinton Road, with extra science laboratories and kitchens put up, and a covered Games Hall and Design Centre at Tipperlin, adjoining the existing PT buildings. Roger Young was to be Principal of the combined school while Hilda Fleming would

have the title of Vice-Principal. With over 2,400 pupils, George Watson's was now the largest co-educational school in Scotland. The move was welcomed by the press, with large headlines such as 'Girls for Watson's Classes', 'Co-ed plan meets warm approval' and the jocular 'Boys. This is a girl'.

Unfortunately, all these promising initiatives took place against a background of mounting concern about the Government's education policies. Although the transfer of pupils from Melville College had helped with the roll numbers at Stewart's Melville, parents and staff alike felt that they were being kept in the dark about what was going to happen, and The Merchant Company realised that they would have to do something about the growing discontent. On 5 February 1975, two thousand parents and members of staff of The Merchant Company schools therefore gathered in a fraught atmosphere at Stewart's Melville College to hear Master Hugh McMaster and William McDonald, the Secretary, explain the Company's position with regard to the current educational crisis.

Three days later, an even larger number of parents who had children at any Edinburgh grant-aided school held an open meeting in the Assembly Hall at the Mound to voice their concerns. Immediately afterwards, a separate meeting of Merchant Company parents took place and The Merchant Company Parents' Association was formed. It had more than 1,000 members and a committee consisting of six parents from each of the three schools. They were able to voice their complaints, but their forebodings intensified on 20 February 1975 when William Ross, Secretary of State for Scotland, announced that integration into the state system would be offered to the grant-aided schools and, on 11 March, made it known that the phasing out of the customary grants to such schools would begin in the 1976–7 session.

Two days after that announcement, The Merchant Company Education Board met to draw up a confidential policy statement summarising the history of the ongoing crisis. Their prime duty, they said, was to preserve and administer the Trusts left by the founders of their three schools, Mary Erskine, George Watson and Daniel Stewart. They must go on providing an education 'for children of a broad range of ability from different backgrounds' and, within the number of places available in the schools, 'allow a degree of parental choice and a flexible form of education'. The problem was how to do this without the vital government grant. They had already had to increase the school fees by 25% at the start of the 1974–5 session, only to be forced to increase them again at the beginning of the summer term because of the unexpected back-dated increase in teacher's salaries recommended in the Houghton Report.

The situation improved slightly when pupils from John Watson's co-educational school combined with The Merchant Company schools. It had been founded by an Edinburgh lawyer who died in 1762, leaving money to set up a refuge for pregnant women, 'assisting them in their delivery so as to conceal their shame and take care of their children as foundlings'. In 1822 it was officially changed into a hospital for destitute children, and later into a school for both boys and girls. It had always been managed by the Writers to the Signet, but in 1975, because of the financial situation, they had to close it. As a result, 136 of their pupils went to George Watson's College, 95 transferred to Mary Erskine's and 85 joined Daniel Stewart's. Their building was then sold and became the Scottish National Gallery of Modern Art.

This obviously benefited the Merchant Company, but it was far from solving the problem, and they felt that they had been

William Ross, Secretary of State for Scotland, 1975 (© RCAHMS Licensor www.rcahms.gov.uk)

presented with only two possible options. They could either go along with the Government's policy and merge their schools with Lothian Region's state comprehensive system, or they could make their schools fully independent – but how could they ever afford to do that? Before they took a final decision, they would have to hold meetings with the other grant-aided schools, the Scottish Education Department and Lothian Regional Council. This they did. They were very much against transferring their schools to the state system, but they simply could not see how to survive as totally independent organisations. Nevertheless, the Education Board members were absolutely determined to find a solution, and after many further discussions they believed that they had identified a compromise. They would dispose of one of their schools to the Region. Its endowments, along with the proceeds from the sale of that school's buildings, would allow the

John Watson's School, 1830, drawn by Thomas H. Shepherd and engraved by W. Watkins, now the Scottish National Gallery of Modern Art (© RCAHMS Licensor www.rcahms.gov.uk)

other two Company schools to survive as 'endowed independents'.

So which school would they sacrifice? They had no intention of losing George Watson's. Not only was it their largest, but as it was now co-educational and was strengthening its all-through policy, the Government would surely allow it to continue as an endowed independent. Stewart's Melville College was also doing well, not only with additional buildings being put up but with very healthy pupil numbers, although of course it was not co-educational. What about Mary Erskine's, however? Comparatively speaking, its roll was small, its ethos as a 'Ladies' College' was out of keeping with current thinking and it seemed to be competing ever more unsuccessfully with the independent St George's School for new pupils. Loth-

ian Region would surely be eager to buy its fine buildings, with their excellent facilities and beautiful setting. The decision was taken. With deep regret, the Company would have to dispose of The Mary Erskine School. At the same time, they would transform Stewart's Melville into a co-educational school. In June, the Education Board wrote to the parents to tell them of the decision.

Needless to say, the letters were received with alarm and dismay. Many wanted nothing to do with co-education and insisted that their daughters must go to a single-sex school. They were horrified by the thought that if they could not find a place for them at another independent school or could not afford to pay its fees, they might have to send their girls to a state school, which was what the Government expected them to do. What-

ever happened, the closure of Mary Erskine's would mean great disruption to the pupils who were there. The Company were equally concerned about that, but their discussions with Lothian Region were friendly and positive and the Region went enthusiastically ahead with plans to borrow £2.75 million from the Government so that they could make the purchase. Everything seemed to be settled when, on 10 December 1975, the Secretary of State announced that the request for the loan had been refused. Lothian Region could not purchase Mary Erskine's.

Why did William Ross block the plan? The official reason given was that there were not enough pupils moving from grant-aided schools to the state sector to justify the Region purchasing an additional building. Later speculation wondered if either the

Government had resented being asked to buy Mary Erskine's rather than simply being given the buildings or if William Ross hoped that, by refusing the loan, he would in the long run force the Education Board to hand over all three schools. Whatever the truth of it, both The Merchant Company and Lothian Region were bitterly disappointed at the collapse of their plan. At first they hoped that they could find another way to progress it. On 9 January 1976 Master McMaster told the Education Board that Lothian Region had agreed to purchase Mary Erskine's from The Merchant Company by way of an annuity agreement, which would allow payment to be spread over 25 years. They had been told that the consent of the Secretary of State was not necessary for this, but they had subsequently discovered that, because such an arrangement

The Scottish National Gallery of Modern Art, formerly John Watson's School (© Ian Watson)

151

The Mary Erskine School at Ravelston in the 1970s (Courtesy of The Mary Erskine School)

came under the heading of capital expenditure, they would have to seek his permission after all. The Region had therefore sent the necessary application to the Scottish Education Department two days earlier.

On 15 January 1976, the Secretary of State announced that he was refusing permission for an annuity agreement. Acknowledging defeat, the Education Board said that they would proceed to full independent status for all three schools and in February they announced that they would launch a Merchant Company's Schools Appeal aimed at raising £1 million. They were by now well aware that they must take the parents and staff of the schools along with them in putting into practice any future plan, for 'the days when parents were grateful to have their children admitted to such schools were over'. They co-opted a member of the Parents' Association to the Education Board and then they set up a Schools Joint Working Party, led by Master McMaster and consisting of the other Company office-bearers and the head teachers, to consider what the future might hold.

Jean Thow, supported by her Vice-Convener John Amour, produced what came to be known as Plan A. This said that Mary Erskine's should become a small, independent, single-sex school, preferably outside The Merchant Company group altogether, with which they now had little in common. If they did continue with the Company, then there should be a different governing body with a bursar to manage the school's finances and its building on a day-to-day basis. Accustomed as they were to their previous careers as heads of independent schools in England, the various Merchant Company head teachers in the past had been used to reporting to a Board of Governors and having a far greater say in policy than they did when they came to Edinburgh and were tied to seeking permission for everything from The Merchant Company Secretary, something which they had all resented to a greater or lesser degree. The Education Board considered Plan A on 17 and 21 May 1976, did not like it and asked to see an alternative proposal.

At their next meeting, on 31 May 1976, the Working Party undertook a very close examination of the Education Board's finances. Most of the realisable assets had been sold to finance the recent capital expenditure at Ravelston, Stewart's Melville and Watson's. This meant that the fees paid by parents and the ever-dwindling government grant were the main sources of income. Watson's was expected to show a surplus in 1977. Stewart's Melville would probably do slightly better than breaking even, but Mary Erskine's would have a deficit of about £60,000. Its position was untenable. The post of Headmaster at Stewart's Melville was currently vacant, for in 1975 Principal Bellis had left to become Headmaster of The Leys School, Cambridge, deploring in his last prize-giving speech what he described as the irreparable damage to the educational system likely to be caused by the Government's policy towards the grant-aided schools. Although the Board had chosen as his successor Robin Morgan, Principal of Campbell College, Belfast, he would not take up his position until 1 January 1977.

Meanwhile, in November 1976, Master McMaster had been succeeded by the meticulous and courteous Kenneth Ryden, who would now have to lead the Company through its educational crisis. Brought up in Blackburn, Lancashire, where he attended Queen Elizabeth's Grammar School and sang in the Cathedral choir, he had joined the Civil Service in 1936 and trained as an estate surveyor with the Ministry of Works. During World War II, he had served in India and Burma with the Royal Bombay Sappers and Engineers, and was awarded the Military Cross with bar. While he was commanding a detachment of Sappers at Yenanyaung in the Mandalay Region of Burma, his armoured column was attacked by the enemy and seven of his men were wounded. Without the slightest hesitation he went into the open three times to recover them. 'This officer's courage, determination and complete disregard for his own safety was an inspiration to all who saw it and is typical of this gallant officer's actions throughout this campaign,' said the citation put forward by the commanding officer of the 3rd Dragoon Guards. This resulted in the award of an immediate

Master Kenneth Ryden (The Merchant Company Archive)

Military Cross to Lieutenant Ryden, the earlier Military Cross won by him at Shwebo being gazetted as a Bar to this new award. After that, he worked for a time in India, where he was involved in the maintenance of the Taj Mahal. Returning to Scotland, in 1959 he founded the Scottish chartered surveyors and property consultants, Kenneth Ryden and Partners, in Hanover Street, Edinburgh.

Once Robin Morgan was in post, the Schools Joint Working Party led by Master Ryden met on 14 June 1977 to consider the latest plan, Plan B, which would offer two possibilities. The first was that Mary Erskine's and Stewart's Melville could merge right away. Because there would obviously be a lot of objections to that, alternatively the Ravelston building could be retained for three years, so that the girls could either finish their course there or it could be arranged for them to be transferred gradually to Watson's or

Stewart's Melville. No new pupils would be admitted to Mary Erskine's and after the three years were up, the school and its site would be sold. Horrified at the idea of Ravelston closing and perturbed at the thought of the disruption to the existing pupils' education, Vice-Convener John Amour wrote what he described as a memorandum, arguing that if any school were to be closed, it should be George Watson's.

By the time the Working Party presented their report to the Education Board on 22 September 1977, they had met seven times. At their final meeting, a vote was taken and the only two members in favour of Plan A were Miss Thow and John Amour. The others all rejected it, apart from Robin Morgan, who sensibly abstained. Instead, they would submit the second course put forward in Plan B to the Education Board for consideration. When that meeting took place, John Amour had already complained bitterly to the Master, who replied that the suggestion that Watson's should be sold was totally unrealistic. In the end, the Board agreed formally with the Working Party that the status quo could not go on, but recognised that there was no easy solution and its own discussions would have to continue.

Meanwhile, the Parents' Association Committee members were working on a paper which they produced on 30 December 1977. An early decision on what was going to happen should be the Education Board's highest priority, they said, for uncertainty was ruining morale and the Board should reaffirm that it meant to preserve the identity of all three schools. They felt that there was no need to be too pessimistic about pupil numbers. The Board had expressed the view that the falling birth rate would reduce applications, but the parents were of the opinion that this affected only working-class families, which were often large, while most

Daniel Stewart's Pipe Band, about 1980 (Courtesy of Stewart's Melville College)

of the existing pupils were from small, middle-class families. Moreover, they believed that parents would continue to make sacrifices to let their children have a good education, and that, with more middle-class women now working outside the home, the income of many school families was rising.

There was another consideration too. The Merchant Company schools were particularly attractive, the parents said, because their academic standards were rooted in the Scottish education system, unlike other independent Edinburgh schools which had their senior pupils sitting English examinations to prepare them for entrance to Oxford and Cambridge. The Company schools should resist the temptation to follow their example

and should not adopt 'an increasingly anglicised emphasis'. In all this, there must be close cooperation with the parents, for the more they were asked to do, the more they would do. Their main aim should not be fund-raising, of course, but helping and supporting the staff, and they might be even more willing to lend a hand if they had access to school facilities such as swimming pools for family activities. They would be willing to pay for that if need be, but the advantage was that this sharing would give them an even greater sense of identity with the schools.

When the Education Board met on 19 January 1978, they noted the Parents' Association Report but dismissed it as being concerned only with general policy, rather than

155

with specific proposals. The parents were certainly unaware of the latest plans and did not yet know that the Education Board had finally come to a decision. It would not sell Mary Erskine's, and it would not turn Stewart's Melville into a completely co-educational school. Instead, there would be a compromise. The junior classes at Mary Erskine's and Stewart's Melville would merge, with primary classes 1–5 based at Stewart's Melville while 6 and 7 would remain at Ravelston as single-sex classes. The senior schools would be twinned, remaining in their own buildings but with their timetables 'harmonised and synchronised' wherever possible. Sixth form subjects taken by only a few pupils would be taught on a joint basis, with the facilities for music, drama, swimming and recreation being shared.

Jean Thow opposed this, for she was against co-education and she wanted to keep all her girls at Ravelston. Robin Morgan was also averse to co-education at this point. Accustomed to a boys-only college, and enthused by military matters in general and his cadet force in particular, he was initially averse to the prospect of giggling little girls invading his masculine world of energetic young warriors. However, he soon realised the advantages of the scheme. By combining the two junior schools there should be an estimated saving of £60,000, while the twinning of the senior schools would also result in considerable savings. The Scottish Education Department would have to be consulted about these plans, of course, and the Parents' Association would be told in confidence at their next committee meeting the following month.

The discussions with the Scottish Education Department went well, but when the parents were told, they were annoyed that they had not been consulted earlier and that their previous paper had not been circulated to Board members before the January meeting. The Merchant Company replied that it had not arrived in time for that to be done. More importantly, the parents insisted that the entire Mary Erskine Junior School must be kept at Ravelston and that nothing must change before August 1979. Jean Thow supported this view, of course, but Robin Morgan was in favour of the Board's plan to implement the merger and the twinning proposals right away and, on 24 February 1978, The Merchant Company Secretary wrote to all the parents to tell them that the Junior Schools merger would take place at the beginning of the 1978–9 session and would be followed by the twinning of the senior schools.

Jean Thow protested that she had not been consulted; but the overriding need to find a solution to the financial problems confronting the Company had, of necessity, been the focus of their discussions, and in any case some parents felt that the atmosphere at Mary Erskine's was far too old-fashioned now. According to them, Miss Thow still seemed to be raising young ladies, rather than modern girls who should have a much wider vision of their role and far greater participation in, for example, outdoor sports and other recreational activities. In June 1978 the Secretary wrote to both head teachers, asking them whether they would be interested in taking up the new appointment of Principal in overall charge of both schools. Robin Morgan replied with alacrity, expressing enthusiasm. Jean Thow did not answer the question, and on 2 October 1978, Morgan was appointed. Afterwards, he joked that he had celebrated his 48th birthday that day, and must be one of the few men in history to be given 800 girls as a birthday present. Jean Thow would be his Vice-Principal.

After that, Robin Morgan spent three days a week at Stewart's Melville and two days a

Margaret Thatcher, Prime Minister (Scottish National Portrait Gallery)

week at Mary Erskine's, in a changed situation which was very difficult for everyone. Principal Morgan took assembly twice a week, interviewed staff and pupils on his two days at Ravelston and urged parents to come to him with their problems. Colonel Sir James Stirling of Garden, one of the business partners of Kenneth Ryden, was Vice-Convener of Mary Erskine's and thought that Morgan handled matters very tactfully. However, the staff and girls felt that they had been sidelined – and instead of being Headmistress, Jean Thow found herself relegated to a subsidiary role with no real authority at all.

At the general election of 4 May 1979, Margaret Thatcher became Prime Minister of the newly elected Conservative Government and financial prospects for the schools eased. In his report at the annual prize-giving that summer Robin Morgan, now an enthusiastic convert to co-education, assured his listeners that The Merchant Company Education Board's new system was satisfactorily in place and that great attention was being paid to the girls' recreational needs. Two of his girls would even be accompanying him to Bisley, he said, where school shooting competitions were a well-known annual event, and there they would undoubtedly disarm the opposition with their attractive ways, 'putting them off their aim'. That summer, Jean Thow resigned. Dignified and earnest, she had preferred not to engage in the sort of charm offensive adopted by her predecessor Muriel Jennings towards male colleagues. Interviewed some years later, Miss Jennings remarked tartly and with not a little self-satisfaction, 'That was where she went wrong!'

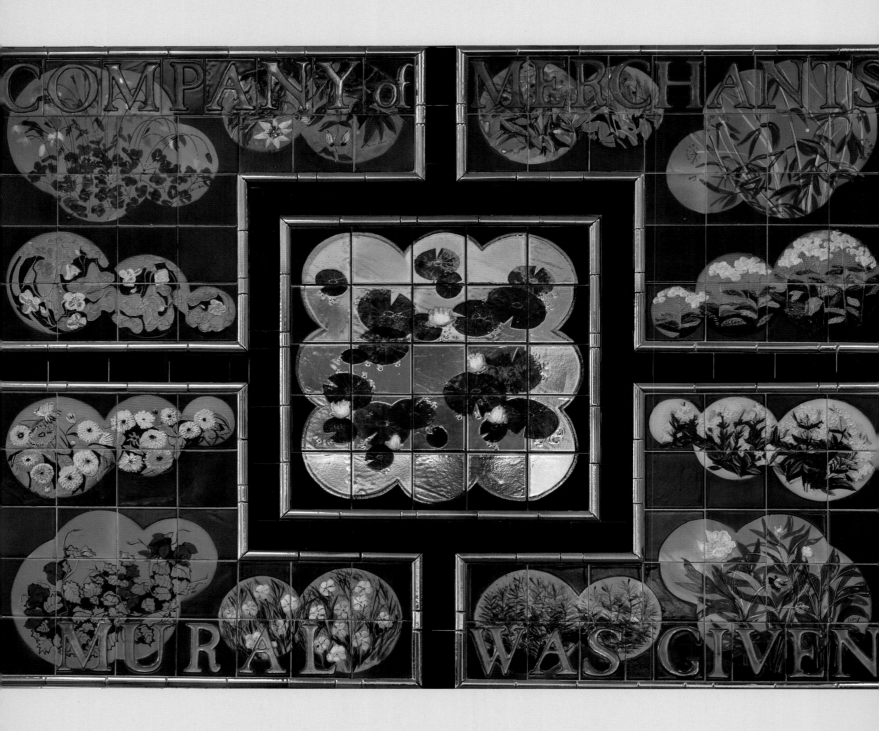

CHAPTER 9

Reconstruction and Innovation: 1982–1999

In 1986 Michael Walker became Master of The Merchant Company. An imposing figure, he was not merely well known for the carnation he always wore in his button hole and for his legendary generosity and thoughtfulness. He also ran the Leith timber business originally founded in Banff by his great-grandfather and, as his colleague and friend Sir Ewan Brown would later recall, his very full life centred on 'the family company, the timber trade both at home and overseas, the Holyrood High Constables, the Western General Hospital and the Royal Warrant Holders – and he still found time for fishing, ski-ing, travelling, dining, music and the theatre'. Moreover, he became, said Sir Ewan, 'the agent of change at the Company and an enormous (I use that word advisedly) influence for good'. So what did he achieve?

In a way, everything seemed to be in a satisfactory enough state when his term of office began. Admittedly, even after the election of a Conservative government in 1979, there had still been concerns about what might happen should it be followed by another Labour administration. The Merchant Company had therefore set up a Contingency Planning Committee to consider what could be done to protect themselves in

such a situation. In the end, however, the emergency plans were not required, for Margaret Thatcher would serve three consecutive terms of office as Prime Minister. In 1981 the Government introduced an Assisted Places scheme to replace the former grant aid system and by 1982–3 The Merchant Company schools were receiving a block grant of £631,200 along with £421,000 under the fee remission scheme. That scheme would last until 1997.

The Education Board had also been able to add to their funds by making some lucrative sales. Belford House was no longer required for boarders at Erskine Stewart's Melville and so it was sold in 1984 for £120,500, and the Education Board proceeded to purchase 11 and 11a Queensferry Terrace the following year. This meant that they now owned all the properties in that street from numbers 3 to 13. On a larger scale, it was decided in 1981 to sell part of the sports ground at Ferryfield. Stewart's Melville had inherited this land from Melville College, with which it had by then merged, and the area had risen immensely in value. A firm of builders could put up housing there, if the necessary planning permission were given. The east section was duly sold to J. Smart &

OPPOSITE.
One of the Marjorie Clinton ceramic mural panels (Courtesy of the Mary Erskine School)

LEFT.
Master Michael Walker (The Merchant Company Archive)

RIGHT.
Master (later Sir) Ewan Brown (The Merchant Company Archive)

Co. (Contractors) for the sum of £1,030,000. In 1987, 5.3 acres of the west section went for £750,000 and in 1996 Wimpey the builders paid £1,892,500 for the remaining 2.648 acres. Part of this, the sum of £607,369, was then passed to the Salvation Army, to clear pre-emption rights that they had over the land next to their property.

During this period, the schools also benefited from several very generous bequests. Henry Convie from Leith had spent most of his life in Canada, in modest circumstances, but accumulating a fortune by way of astute investments. In 1985 he left his entire estate of £270,000 to George Watson's College. He was not a former pupil, but when he was young he had always gazed admiringly and not a little enviously at the handsome buildings and the pupils in their smart maroon uniforms. He had taken an interest in the school ever since. The following year, Norman Hyde, a former music master at Watson's, left £15,000 to the school's music department and, a year after that, Jessie Manning, once a pupil of Watson's Ladies' College, bequeathed to Watson's £50,000, an eighth of the residue of her estate. All this was reassuring, but Master Walker's vision for the future was not that things should simply go on as they were. The time had come, he believed, to look again at the way the Company was run, so that the membership would continue to grow and the schools would evolve and flourish.

One of his principal concerns was that the large administrative staff required for running the schools were all in the Merchant Company Hall in Hanover Street. Not only

Gates from Melville College's playing fields at Ferryfield, now located at the Erskine Stewart's Melville playing fields at Inverleith (Photograph © Ian Watson)

did this mean that the Hall's offices were cramped and overcrowded, but it was also geographically awkward, since the schools were in the suburbs of the city. More importantly, the current arrangement was restricting the natural development of the schools. This had long caused considerable dissatisfaction among the various head teachers over the years. We have seen how Robert Robertson, the Mary Erskine Headmaster, had to exchange long letters with Alexander Heron every day at the beginning of the twentieth century and how Muriel Jennings resented the supervisory role of H.M. Harvey-Jamieson in the 1950s. More recently, Mrs Bellis, the wife of the Stewart's Melville Principal, once told his successor, Patrick Tobin, that she finally decided that her husband must resign when he was asked to send his annual prize-giving speech in advance to the Company's Deputy Secretary for his approval.

Their discontent was far from being the sole cause of Master Walker's desire for reform, of course. He was convinced that the schools could be much more efficiently run if power were devolved to them, putting them in charge of their own buildings and finances. Of course they would always have to operate within the budgets and policies laid down by the Education Board but, as Patrick Tobin remarked, Master Walker had realised that the schools would never reach their full potential unless they were able to 'fashion their individual destinies'. Education apart, there were other vital questions to consider too. Was the current structure of The Merchant Company really appropriate for present times, or should it be reorganised?

Master Douglas Kinloch Anderson (The Merchant Company Archive)

and consisted of Ewan Brown (Director of Noble Grossart, the well-known merchant bank) and three of The Merchant Company Assistants: Geoffrey Ball, Frank Kidd and Sandy Orr. They were instructed to discuss a wide range of concerns and make recommendations covering five main areas. These were the future structure of the Company, the optimum number of committees, membership and social aspects and, last but certainly not least, a programme for radical change in the administration of the schools. The Steering Group duly began their discussions, and it rapidly became obvious that those subjects were linked in many different ways. Moreover, there were three major factors which were fundamental to the need for the review they were undertaking. These were the recent changes in the area of education, the altered needs and priorities of members as a result of general social and economic developments in Britain, and the desirability of widening the members' involvement in Company business. The Group decided that they could best consider these matters under two headings, educational and non-educational.

Who should sit on the important Education and Endowments Boards? For how long should office-bearers serve, and was there some way in which their expertise might be used after their terms of office had expired? How many committees and sub-committees should there be? There were far too many at present, involving endless meetings, all too often attended by the very same small group of members. What was the best way to recruit new members, and how could they be given a real feeling of belonging to a community? Underlying everything else, of course, was the vital question of how best to increase the Company finances.

In pursuit of answers, Master Walker in 1987 set up a small Steering Group. It was led by Douglas Kinloch Anderson (Chairman of Kinloch Anderson, tailors and kilt-makers),

The Steering Group Report was completed early the following year and, on 4 February 1988, Master Walker summarised it when he addressed the Company's Stated General Meeting that day. To look first at their educational recommendations, he had, of course, chosen like-minded colleagues to serve on the Steering Group, and they now proposed that significant responsibility for the running of the schools should be devolved to two school Governing Boards: one for Mary Erskine's and Stewart's Melville on the north side of the city, and the other for George Watson's on the south side. Each Governing Board would have 12 Governors who would be able to fix the level of its school's fees and control their operational budgets, their property and their assets. The schools would have a full-time bursar and/or secretary and clerk of works, with adequate support staff. The Governing Boards would be chaired by a Merchant Company member and would include Governors with financial, property and legal expertise, along with one who was involved with the Former Pupils' Clubs or one who was a parent. The Principal and the Bursar would attend all meetings of the Board of Governors.

In spite of plans to devolve considerable power to the schools themselves, the Education Board had no intention of abdicating its own responsibilities. It would continue to have a highly important role. While it was vital 'that the real executive power and practical decision-making rests with the school Governing Boards', said the Report, the Education Board 'must retain its strategic role and have certain reserve powers'. It would review long-term educational strategy and the relationship between the various Company schools. It would administer the educational trusts, approve the proposed annual budget and the annual accounts of each Governing Board, the sale or purchase of major assets, the appointment of new Principals and of the two Governing Boards Chairmen. The Master of The Merchant Company would himself chair the Education Board, which would include the Treasurer, an Old Master, the two chairmen of the Governing Boards, and four current Assistants. There would be one representative from the District Council, one from the Regional Council and one from the Church of Scotland's Presbytery of Edinburgh, along with two co-opted members.

On the same day that Master Walker addressed The Merchant Company's Stated General Meeting, he held a meeting of the Education Board and outlined the Steering Group's proposals to its members. Robin

Frank Gerstenberg, Principal of George Watson's College (Courtesy of George Watson's College)

Morgan and Frank Gerstenberg, now the Principal of Watson's College, were in attendance. Gerstenberg, a Scot, was a Cambridge graduate in history and had previously been Headmaster of Oswestry School, an independent, co-educational day and boarding school on the border of England and Wales. He had succeeded Sir Roger Young in 1985. Both he and Principal Morgan listened carefully and then commented. In their previous schools they had both been accustomed to working with the sort of arrangements proposed, they said, and they welcomed the concept of greater devolution to the schools.

Principal Gerstenberg added that he hoped that further thought would be given to the composition of the Governing Boards with regard to the need for female members and parental representation. Similarly, The Merchant Company Parents' Association representative hoped that a parent would indeed be one of the co-opted members and that a minimum number of Governors should be parents. In the end, it was agreed that each Governing Board would consist of three co-opted members of the Education Board, four of its Assistants and five other co-opted members, who might or might not be members of that Board. After further lengthy discussions, the Report was approved and the

Steering Group was transformed into an Implementation Committee, chaired by Master Walker himself.

Making the changes was, of course, no simple matter, for various legal formalities were necessary. It was not until October 1989 that the Court of Session granted the formal petition required to establish the two Governing Councils (as the new Boards would be known) and, at the end of the year, the administrative staff moved out of the Merchants' Hall to the schools. Michael Walker had completed his term of office as Master the previous November and was succeeded by Sir Peter Heatly, a civil engineer, who was not only chairman of his own company but a famous diver who had competed in the Olympics and had won several Commonwealth Games gold medals. As Treasurer, he had been extremely supportive of the Steering Group plans.

Old Master Walker did not give up his educational activities, however, for he now became Chairman of the Governing Council of the North Side and, when Robin Morgan retired, Walker determinedly secured as Principal of Erskine Stewart's Melville Patrick Tobin, an Oxford graduate and previously Principal of Prior Park, a boys' boarding school in Bath. Old Master Walker had taken soundings about a suitable candidate, visited Tobin in Bath, and struck up a rapport with him. Sir Ewan Brown would later observe that, as the first chairman of Erskine Stewart's Melville's Governing Council, Walker's greatest triumph was 'the relentless pursuit and landing of the person, Patrick Tobin, he wanted to run these schools as Principal'. Tobin, for his part, would remember Michael Walker with admiration, remarking that 'it is rare for a man so effortlessly to combine wisdom and gravitas with such puckish fun and enjoyment of life'.

The new regime firmly in place, George

Patrick Tobin, Jean Thow and Robin Morgan on the occasion of Mary Erskine's School's tercentenary, 1994 (Courtesy of Stewart's Melville College)

Watson's held a double celebration in 1991, for the 250th anniversary of Watson's Hospital and the 120th anniversary of the Ladies' College. The school had recently launched an appeal which would bring in more than its £1 million target. The proceeds were used for a new Technology Centre, which was opened in 1993, and a major refurbishment of the Design Centre. In 1994 Mary Erskine's marked its tercentenary by setting up an appeal for a new Sixth Form Centre and pavilion, and Founder's Day was attended by the formerly warring Jean Thow and Robin Morgan, who were even photographed together, with Patrick Tobin. The Former Pupils' Guild held a special dinner at the Balmoral Hotel attended by 359 women and seven men, and they presented the school with a fine ceramic mural by Marjorie Clinton, showing herbs known to have been grown in Edinburgh Physic Garden around the time when Mary Erskine was running her second husband's apothecary business.

Devolution of authority to the schools was a resounding success, and the Principals and staff were well satisfied with the new arrangements. The pupils, while they obviously noticed the arrival of the administrative staff in their buildings, were probably less aware of the changes. For them, particularly the younger ones, the day-to-day dramas of the classroom and the sports field took precedence over everything else, and the role of The Merchant Company itself rarely entered their consciousness. Elizabeth Cumming, who later became a distinguished art historian, had been a pupil at George Watson's Ladies' College. When she was still very young, her parents asked her as usual one day what she had been doing. The school had in fact been visited by the Vice-Convener, a role which continued until 1994. Elizabeth's parents were convulsed with laughter when she thought for a moment and then replied innocently, 'Well, we had a visit from the Vice-Cleaner.'

The departure of the schools' administrative staff from Hanover Street meant that much more of the Hall was available for other activities, and this had implications for several of the new sub-committees set up as a result of the Steering Group Report. It had recommended that the traditional composition of the Master's Court ought to be retained, but it also suggested setting up four new sub-committees: Property and Finance; Charitable Activities; Industry and Education Liaison; and Membership and Social Matters. The Property and Finance Committee were obviously involved in the question of repairs and maintenance of the Hall, while the Membership and Social Matters Committee were eager to increase the involvement of existing members as well as attracting new ones. They therefore agreed that the Merchants' Hall should become a centre for social and civic activities, with lectures, receptions and other events arranged specially for the membership. Obviously, the Hall's main rooms would have to be re-decorated in an up-to-date but

One of the Marjorie Clinton ceramic mural panels (Courtesy of the Mary Erskine School)

dignified manner and a well-equipped kitchen, cloakroom and lavatories were very necessary. These improvements would encourage more outside organisations to hire rooms for their events, thus bringing in additional money, and they would also make them more attractive for the members' own gatherings.

A scheme of general refurbishment had been completed in 1984 by Simpson Decor Ltd, but a complete redecoration of the rooms had not been possible at that time because it would have been too expensive. Even more expensive roof repairs had of necessity distracted attention from the interior. These went on for more than six years, and included the replacement of the glass in the dome. In 1987 the general refurbishment of 18 Hanover Street was approved at an estimated cost of £5,400, and the hire fees were then increased. Use of the hall for dinners for up to 150 people would cost £160, with an extra £50 for access to the kitchen facilities. Receptions for as many as 250 were available for £120, and meetings for up to 170 people would cost £100 for a full day. The Court

Room could be hired for smaller receptions of up to 80 people or meetings of no more than 40. The hire fee was the same for each type of event: £60 for a full day, £50 for a half day or evening. Voluntary and charitable organisations would be charged only half the usual rate.

There had recently been changes in the Hall's tenants, too, with the Clydesdale Bank moving their Princes Street branch to 20 Hanover Street in 1985, and Kelly Services, the recruitment company, taking premises in number 24 when Kodak departed two years later. It was unfortunate that a structural engineer had advised leaving the top floor of 18 Hanover Street empty, explaining that the floor loadings were inadequate for normal use, and it was regrettable that the Carnegie Trust in 1992 left the offices they had occupied since 1901. These vacancies resulted in a shortfall in the annual rental income of the £14,500 which had previously been charged for the top floor of number 18, as well as £16,000 for the Carnegie Trust offices. In spite of the losses, however, in 1992 the Treasurer recommended that a fund should be set up which would enable a much-needed further programme of refurbishment and redecoration to begin. This was delayed, partly by necessary repairs to the Rose Street Lane area, but in 1995 the redecoration of the hall was authorised during the Mastership of Ewan Brown and the Court Room was improved by the repair of blinds, carpets and curtains.

Various other works had to be carried out to satisfy fire safety regulations, arguments continued about the floor loading capacity at number 18 and in 1997 a much-needed new sound system was installed in the hall. In November, Gilbert Baird Archer became Master. His long and successful business career had included terms of office as President of Edinburgh Chamber of Commerce, Deputy President of the British Chambers of Com-

ABOVE.
Master Gilbert Baird Archer
(The Merchant Company
Archive)

OPPOSITE.
The Merchants' Hall interior,
watercolour by Hugh
Buchanan (The Merchant
Company; painting © Hugh
Buchanan; photograph ©
John McKenzie photography)

merce, Master of the Worshipful Company of Gunmakers (a London livery company) and Moderator of the High Constables of the Port of Leith; and he would also become Deputy Lieutenant of Peeblesshire. During his term as Master, display cases were placed in the original bank vault where the valuable treasures are kept, making it possible for the contents to be viewed by special guests who are given the privilege of being allowed in to admire them.

John Amour, the former Vice-Convener of Mary Erskine's, was then appointed Company Archivist. His duties were not those of an ordinary archivist, in that he would not spend his time cataloguing the archives. Instead, he would assist in insurance valuations, security of the valuables and the presentation and promotion of the precious archives, which date back to the Middle Ages. Almost everything was ready in time for the December 1999 Members' Dinner. Even the famous silver gilt ship centrepiece had been repaired by Hamilton and Inches, for it had been noticed that its mast needed to be straightened, some of the rigging replaced and the flags adjusted.

By that time, an interesting increase in

Ms Dawn Burrows, first woman member of the Merchant Company since the seventeenth century (© Peter Mennim)

membership had taken place. On 21 October 1993, Dawn Burrows of Burrows & Company Ltd had become the first woman to be admitted as an ordinary member of The Merchant Company for almost three hundred years. Quite why there had been this long interlude remains a mystery, for there never seems to have been a ban on businesswomen becoming members and, as we have seen, there were several in the years immediately following the 1681 Charter. For some unknown reason the practice of admitting them just seems to have faded away. From her childhood, Dawn Burrows had been aware of the Company, for her father was a member and she herself attended one of The Merchant Company schools. She was always interested in the Company's activities and, when she grew up and was involved in her family's woollen business, she felt sorry that she was not eligible to join. By 1990, however, all that was about to change.

The sub-committee known as the Membership and Social Group had duly been set up after the Steering Group's deliberations, and there were now just over 700 Company members. All of them were men, until a member's wife expressed an interest in becoming a Company member herself. The Group were

receptive to the idea and concluded that, because she was involved in business, there would be no difficulty in processing an application from her. Of course the terms of the Widows' Fund would have to be altered to indicate that 'a male could mean the female in descriptions', but that was easy enough to arrange. The Group decided to make the question of female membership a priority, and Master Douglas Kinloch Anderson supported the idea. He was a former pupil of George Watson's and a graduate of St Andrews University, his tailoring and tartans firm had been founded in 1868 and he was not only the fifth generation of his family to run the business, but his grandfather had been Master of The Merchant Company. As well as his many other interests, he had recently been President of the Edinburgh Royal Warrant Holders Association and had just served as President of Edinburgh Chamber of Commerce when he became Master.

The Master's Court accordingly took up the notion of admitting women members, and by 12 November 1992, Master Kinloch Anderson was telling the Annual General Meeting that the Company felt that there must be many more men and women who were qualified to join. He added, 'I said deliberately men and women.' It must be remembered, he added, that one of the earliest benefactors was Mary Erskine, not to mention the fact that almost half of the 4,500 young people at the Company schools were of the female sex and many would enter the world of business and commerce. Those suitably qualified should therefore be encouraged to apply for membership. The Master's Court were a little nervous about the possibility of unqualified people applying and so the Treasurer emphasised at their meeting on 28 January 1993 that female applicants in particular must be occupants of executive positions, for the first group to be admitted

would obviously serve as a pattern for the future. The Membership and Social Group would conduct the interviews, so that they could make sure that standards were upheld. Likewise, they must be seen to be even-handed between male and female applicants and therefore everyone who applied must be questioned in person.

Dawn Burrows sent in her application as soon as her father told her the good news that women were now eligible for membership and, when she was interviewed by the Membership and Social Advisory Committee on 23 March 1993, she had no difficulty in satisfying them as to her credentials. Because of the Widows' Fund regulations, she had to undergo a medical examination, and she later recalled with wry amusement that she was asked, 'Do you smoke . . . cigarettes, cigars, a pipe?' Later she could not recall her response, but told a colleague, 'Knowing me as you do, you will be able to make a fairly accurate guess as to its gist!' There were no more medicals for lady members after that. By this time the Company had decided that they must be proactive in recruiting women, and they drew up a list of likely candidates who might be approached. Some responded enthusiastically while others declined. The next to be

admitted were Helen Jane Hall, who ran Jane Davidson, the exclusive ladies' designer clothes shop originally in Edinburgh's Grassmarket before it moved to Thistle Street, and Judy Wagner, the recruitment executive with Finlayson Wagner Black. Women members continued to be elected and in 1998 Margaret Allan, Director/Company Secretary of Bruce Lindsay Brothers Ltd., became the first woman on the Court for 300 years when she was appointed as an Assistant. As to honorary members, in 1997 The Princess Royal had accepted an invitation to join them, following the example of her mother, The Queen, and her grandmother, Queen Elizabeth The Queen Mother, while the next year Lady Marion Fraser was the first non-royal lady to be added to that distinguished list.

Throughout this period of reconstruction, The Merchant Company's other main charitable activity was also undergoing a transformation. Society's attitudes towards the care of the elderly had been changing, and the Company were aware that they would have to take this into consideration. There were also financial difficulties. Both the Spylaw Street cottages and the Fraser Homes were proving to be increasingly expensive to maintain, and the Company's

LEFT TO RIGHT.

Mrs Helen Jane Hall
(Private collection)

Mrs Judy Wagner (© Steven Parry Donald Photography)

Mrs Margaret Allan, as first woman Secretary of The Merchant Company (The Merchant Company Archive)

Lady Marion Fraser, first non-royal female Honorary Member of the Merchant Company, with her husband, Sir William Fraser (© Steven Parry Donald Photography)

charitable committees were in 1990 considering their future. In keeping with current thinking, it was felt by some members that, with people living longer, it would be better to consider setting up an imaginative new community for the elderly rather than simply paying out pensions or keeping going what had originally been alms houses. In a proper retirement complex the residents could enjoy company, comfortable circumstances and necessary support as they grew increasingly frail. At the same time this would remove a continuing financial drain on the Company's resources. It was true that in 1990 the Endowments Trust had benefited from a legacy of over £200,000 from Robert A. Murray, but even that had not solved the problem.

When a full survey in 1990 showed that at Spylaw Street the estimated cost of the maintenance needed was £47,537, the Endowments Trust decided that the cottages would have to be sold. The first to be put on the market was number 17, bringing in £33,109. Three years later, number 8 went for £43,277, and over the years the sales continued as the cottages fell vacant. The situation at the Fraser Homes was rather different, because they were not separate cottages lining a street but were grouped round a large garden, and because the Sir William Fraser Trustees were involved. However, it was found necessary to undertake a three-year programme of external repairs to roofs, chimney stacks and defective rendering, along with minor plumbing and electrical work.

Once that was done, the Endowments Trust in 1993 made an initial commitment of £50,000 for damp-proofing, rewiring, more plumbing and the conversion of the meeting hall and laundry room into an additional house. Three of the houses were empty by that time, but the Fraser Trustees were unhappy about the Endowments Trust's suggestion that these should be let to commer-

cial tenants. Instead, the Fraser Trustees indicated that they might be prepared to transfer some of their Trust funds to The Merchant Company, on condition that the money would be used for the accommodation and welfare of the residents of the homes. They would make a contribution of £50,000 towards the refurbishment of the houses, they said, and they could consider contributing the balance of their capital at a later stage in the refurbishment programme.

The Endowments Trust accepted the arrangement, agreeing that two of the Fraser Trustees (the Lord Lyon and the Professor of Scottish History and Paleography at Edinburgh University) should attend meetings of the Endowment Trust for the discussion of business relating to the homes. The Fraser Trustees would also retain their right to nominate the occupants of six of the 13 houses. The upgrading programme and the intended roof repairs were finally completed in 1996 at a cost of £95,338, excluding VAT, more than £4,000 less than the original estimate, but it was then found that the west wing roof would have to be repaired at an estimated price of £32,434. Other maintenance work delayed these repairs, and in December 1997 the Fraser Trustees finally resolved to wind up their Trust and transfer their funds, amounting to over £31,000, to The Merchant Company Endowments Trust. The following year, the centenary of the Sir William Fraser Trust was celebrated with a successful if rainy garden party at the Fraser Homes. Meanwhile, in 1993 the Endowments Trust had added to their funds by finally selling for over £275,000 the flats at Drumsheugh Place which had been rented out to Edinburgh University.

By then, Pitsligo House was also giving cause for concern. In 1987 the Private and Voluntary Establishment Social Work Department had put in a very complimentary report about the home and how well it was being

The Fraser Homes (© Steven Parry Donald Photography)

run. However, developers in the private sector were now erecting many new sheltered housing complexes and retirement flats and, two years later, there was not one name on the customary waiting list for accommodation at Pitsligo House. Moreover, its rooms were not suited to those residents who needed additional nursing care. An annual inspection at the end of 1992 showed that there were 45 residents in Pitsligo House, with an average age of 85. The majority used walking aids, but 30 of them were still able to go out unaccompanied, though of course all were inevitably becoming frailer. The oldest was aged 97, five were registered blind, two were deaf and two had slight dementia. The home was running at a loss, despite the fact that charges had been raised more than once and in 1990 stood at £168 a week, and the situation was complicated by the fact that much more stringent regulations affecting care homes had been brought in. The following year, Lothian Social Work Department were again commenting on the high standard of accommodation and care at Pitsligo House, but the Endowments Trust felt that they had to advise The Merchant Company that it should be sold. They simply did not have the funds to modify it for current nursing care requirements.

The Master's Court recognised the difficulties, but they were reluctant to dispose of the home. The residents would be desperately disappointed and there could very well be adverse publicity. In January 1996 the Endowments Trust were wondering whether to set up a Friends of Pitsligo organisation to help to improve matters, but the following month an estimate for over £34,000 worth of necessary maintenance work came in. The year after that, there were seven rooms vacant and the Company had ascertained that there would be no problem with finding accommodation for the remaining residents if they had to move out. The annual financial losses were steadily increasing, and in 2000 the decision was finally taken, with much regret: Pitsligo House would have to be sold. The residents were indeed dismayed, as was Robin Wilson, The Merchant Company Secretary, when he was told what was to happen. Twelve years earlier, as an Assistant, he had been instructed to assure the elderly ladies that they would never have to move, and some of these same ladies were still there. It was a difficult situation, but they were found other homes, Pitsligo House was put on the market, and the price received for it was approximately £3,250,000.

CHAPTER 10

Towards the Future:
2001–2014

The sale of Pitsligo House did not put an end to The Merchant Company's care for the elderly. Far from it. The proceeds enabled the Endowments Trust to embark upon a whole new programme of development. This came at an interesting time. In 2002 The Princess Royal became the first ever female Master of The Merchant Company. The Princess, like her father, agreed to be Master for one year only, but she regularly attended meetings, was thoroughly conversant with everything that was going on and provided not only wise counsel and advice but ideas for discussion. With the permission of The Queen, The Princess hosted a highly successful charity dinner in the Palace of Holyroodhouse for the Company, and she sat for her striking portrait to Norman Edgar, who had studied at Glasgow School of Art and was famous for his use of strong, bold colours. She unveiled the painting in the hall on 24 February 2004.

The Treasurer in 2003 was Brian Adair. A former pupil of George Watson's and a chartered surveyor, he had been Senior Partner of Ryden's, now one of Scotland's largest privately owned commercial surveying firms. On his retirement in 1989 he became Managing Director of Ryden Lettings, which he had founded, and he was also Chairman of

Trustees of the Royal Scots Club. With his professional expertise he was particularly well placed to give advice on the investment of the Pitsligo House funds. After careful discussions, the Endowments Trust decided to use the money to purchase a large, four-storey block of offices at the east end of Albany Street in Edinburgh. This property cost £4,500,000 and it was acquired with the help of a loan from The Merchant Company Widows' Fund. It was already leased to Messrs Price Waterhouse Cooper Lybrand and sublet to Simpson and Marwick, a well-known firm of Edinburgh solicitors. Its annual rent of £330,000 transformed the finances of the Endowments Trust. So what would they now do with their greatly enhanced funds?

One day, a young charity worker came to see Brian Adair in the context of his letting business, and described to him how her charity was trying to find housing for people who were elderly and disabled. Afterwards it occurred to Master Adair (as he now was) that The Merchant Company should perhaps consider letting out some of its properties for just such a purpose. That would allow the Endowments Trust to carry on the work of Dr Jack Martin in a very appropriate way. However, the Company did not own any

suitable building at that time. Also, bearing in mind the financial difficulties experienced by Pitsligo House, the necessarily very strict regulations now imposed by the Government on care homes and the requirement for expert staff to be employed there, The Merchant Company decided that they could not themselves run a residence for the elderly. They simply did not have anyone suitably qualified in this highly specialised area. Instead, they might be able to enter into a partnership with a firm which could undertake the actual management of a home for the elderly. In 2005, the Trust therefore began to look for a possible site.

It seemed that the Government was willing to give large grants to such projects, and the Endowments Trust learned that there was a possibility of setting up a joint venture with Outlook Housing Association to build 15 housing units for frail and elderly residents on a site in Corstorphine. In the end, Outlook

Housing received such a large contribution from Housing Association Grant Funding that they decided to proceed on their own. However, the investigations into this scheme had provided the Endowments Trust with useful information about how such a project might be carried forward, and The Merchant Company set up a Frail and Elderly Committee to explore the possibility of sharing a project with Dunedin Canmore Housing Association. The new committee was chaired by Jim Gray, a chartered quantity surveyor whose knowledge and experience made him an ideal person to oversee the future building work. The members of the committee were equally well suited to the task: Old Master Adair; Mike Afshar, Chairman of the Property Committee; David Ferguson, Chairman of the Charity Committee; and Alistair Beattie, The Merchant Company Secretary and Chamberlain.

The choice of site was influenced by the

The Merchant Company Master Court, 2003, with Brian Adair as Master and The Princess Royal in her robes as Lord Dean of Guild (© Steven Parry Donald Photography)

conviction that the flats for the elderly should be in a central location, so that the residents would not feel isolated, but would be part of a larger community. AMA were carrying out a development at Springfield, Fountainbridge, an area which had formerly been occupied by Scottish and Newcastle Breweries. A site on the south side of Brandfield Street there was available for social housing, and Dunedin Canmore Housing Association were interested. The Endowments Trust decided to form a partnership with them, purchasing the site and then leasing the property to Dunedin Canmore who, for a specific period of years, would provide

housing support and management. The new retirement complex, six storeys high, would be built by Messrs BAM Construction, who had recently put up the large Interpoint finance block in the Haymarket district of Edinburgh. At Brandfield Street, there would be 40 self-contained flats in all, 20 of which would be financed by The Merchant Company. Nine would have one bedroom, there would be nine others with two bedrooms, two more special flats on the ground floor would be for disabled residents and there would be a common room for residents on the top floor.

The finance for the project would consist

of the Trust's own funds, a Special Needs Capital Grant from the Edinburgh City Council and a bank loan. As Master Adair later remarked, 'The development of these flats was not looked on as an investment. It was a way of providing housing for people in desperate need. We could have spent our money on pensions or grants for the poor and needy, but building such flats seemed a very much more efficient way of distributing our funds and helping a housing sector for which there was a considerable demand.' He suggested that the building should be named 'Jack Martin House', in memory of the generous benefactor who had given the Company Pitsligo House in the first place, and his colleagues welcomed the idea. It was all the more suitable because the Martin family bakery had been situated very near at hand.

The total spent on constructing the flats was £2,309,099 and The Princess Royal formally opened the building on 13 October 2009. Three special plaques were put up in the foyer, one marking the occasion, one commemorating Dr Martin and the other giving information about The Merchant Company. By the end of April 2010 the flats were fully occupied and, two months later, the Planning Department of Edinburgh City Council visited the building and pronounced themselves very impressed. Indeed, one of the Councillors said that the Council would be very likely to look favourably upon The Merchant Company if it were to propose a similar project in the future. This was all very encouraging, the Merchant Company Almoner Dorothy MacLaughlin proved to be very popular with the residents.

Delighted with the success of Brandfield Street, The Merchant Company in the spring of 2011 were considering a number of possible locations for a new development for the frail and elderly, led by Dunedin Canmore. A site owned by Edinburgh City Council in Little

Road, next to Liberton Gardens, seemed the most likely, for the Council already had in place an agreement to sell it to Dunedin Canmore. A grant of £880,000 was secured from the Council and it was agreed that, on completion, Dunedin Canmore would sell the land and the buildings to the Endowments Trust, which would lease it back to them for 30 years. Originally the plan had been for two blocks of flats, with 24 units in all, but in the end the Company managed to have this increased to a total of 48 flats, by repositioning the properties. On 1 May 2013 a reception was held to mark the completion of the legal stages of the complicated process, by which

TOP.
The Princess Royal opening Jack Martin House (The Merchant Company Archive)

ABOVE.
Master Ian Watson (far right) and Mike Afshar (far left) visiting the construction site at Little Road (Photograph courtesy of The Maverick Photo Agency)

TOP.
Merchants' Court, the Little
Road flats (© Ian Watson)

ABOVE.
The Princess Royal opening
the Merchants' Court flats
(© Steven Parry Donald
Photography)

by then realised that there was an opportunity to expand the project further. A strip of land had been left for future development at the Liberton Gardens front of the Little Road site, and there was space for two buildings of three storeys high to be constructed there. J. Smart & Co., the contractor, was enthusiastic about the idea of a Phase 2 and it seemed likely that the City Council might give a further grant. The total cost looked to be between £1.5 million and £2 million, and the Master's Court decided to go ahead. Sixteen more flats would be built as soon as Phase 1 was completed. By the summer of 2014 the 32 flats, now known as Merchants' Court, were not only finished but occupied. The Princess Royal performed the official opening ceremony on 9 September, and Master Ian Watson presented her with a cashmere scarf in the newly commissioned Merchant Company tartan. Work on the further 16 flats followed.

While these exciting developments were taking place, The Merchant Company had not forgotten its existing commitments to the elderly. A celebration of rather a different kind had been held in 2010, when the Endowments Trust organised a very special birthday lunch in the Merchants' Hall – Sam Martinez, their oldest pensioner, reached the age of 100 in May. He had come to Scotland from Belize 68 years earlier, during World War II, and found work felling trees in the Ullapool area. Afterwards, he moved to Edinburgh, married a Scottish girl and settled down to raise a family. He was employed for 25 years at the Balerno Paper Mill but he had no intention of retiring, and he worked on at a butcher's until he was in his late eighties. More than 300 people came to his birthday celebrations, and Master Kennedy Dalton said, 'Sam is an inspiration to us all and, as our oldest beneficiary, we couldn't let this important birthday pass unmarked. Each

time building work had already begun and, thanks to the good weather, was ahead of schedule.

Rapid progress followed. By the beginning of October, 90% of the internal finishings had been selected, Dunedin Canmore had a promising list of potential tenants and the building was expected to be wind and watertight by the middle of November. Mike Afshar, now Chairman of The Merchant Company's Frail and Elderly Committee, had

year he comes along to our Christmas party and is the life and soul of the proceedings. He has spent his life working hard and contributing to life in Edinburgh. It is a privilege for The Merchant Company to be in a position to support Sam and others to have the quality of life they deserve.'

In 2013 the Trust was helping a total of 235 pensioners and contributing £10,000 for the purchase of household appliances and other items for those in need, with the Life-Care almoner employed to deal with such matters on behalf of the Trust. As for the Widows' Fund, it had closed to new members with the Westminster Parliament's Edinburgh Merchant Company Order Confirmation Act (1996). That meant, of course, that the Fund itself was now dwindling, since annual payments to the widowed were still being made. By the time of the Annual General Meeting in November 2013, there were 180 people receiving pensions from the Widows' Fund, and its Trustees agreed to increase

the annual rate from £1,700 to £1,825. The yearly Christmas coffee morning held in the Hanover Street Hall for Merchant Company pensioners was always a happy occasion, and that year more than 70 people attended. Donald Wilson, the Lord Provost of Edinburgh, chatted to all the pensioners, and children from Erskine Stewart's Melville sang carols, which were much enjoyed.

The economic recession in the first decade of the twenty-first century inevitably affected The Merchant Company's investments, and by 2009 another of its charities, the Alexander Darling Silk Mercer's Trust, had run into difficulties. As we saw, Darling's bequest was for elderly women 'of good character', preferably connected with the manufacture or sale of women's and children's clothing. In April 2009 it was recognised that the Darling Trust's expenditure would exceed its income. It supported 68 beneficiaries, and so the Master's Court agreed that the Endowments Trust should make a donation at the end of the year to cover any deficit. Even so, the Darling Trust had to be closed to new members for the time being. However, in late 2009, the Master's Court decided that the Company's investment portfolio and the Widows' Fund should both employ investment managers, and that improved the situation. By 2012 the Endowments Trust had a sufficient surplus to take the decision to increase the number of Darling Trust beneficiaries beyond the previous maximum number of 40.

Meanwhile, the Company's commitment to the young was, as always, a major preoccupation, even though the devolution of the schools' administrative functions was recognised as being a great success. In 2005 the Scottish Parliament passed The Charities and Trustee Investment (Scotland) Act and, as a result, the Office of the Scottish Charity Regulator (OSCR) was set up as a non-ministerial department of the Scottish Administration. The Education Board had registered as a charity, and so now its members found that as charity trustees they were responsible to OSCR each year for their management procedures and accounting. For some time they had been concerned that their charitable status could be in danger if one of the schools suffered financial problems, and so the Master's Court had decided that the two schools should become two independent charitable companies owned by the Board. However, putting that into effect had to be delayed, because OSCR did not at that point know whether it had the power to approve a change of that nature. The Board also felt that its constitution was very much out of date and should be revised, but any alterations to a charity's constitution had to be agreed by OSCR.

After many legal discussions and lengthy delays, the Education Board were in February 2009 re-writing their entire constitution, but

in November 2010 they resigned themselves to the fact that trying to set up three separate charities instead of one was proving far too difficult. The Education Board would have to remain as a single legal entity. However, the constitution still needed to be updated. In the spring of 2011 the draft was sent to OSCR, and on 3 November 2011 the Education Board held a special meeting. OSCR had finally approved the new constitution, and it was adopted with immediate effect. Apart from anything else, this meant that the Principals of George Watson's and Erskine Stewart's Melville would now become members of the new Education Board.

While all these protracted negotiations were in progress, the schools themselves were going from strength to strength. George Watson's decided to introduce the new International Baccalaureate examination in the session 2011–12, appointing five new teachers for the special courses and improving the school's community services, which were an important part of the Baccalaureate. The pupils certainly found it a worthwhile challenge. It was hard work, one of the first batch of those sitting the examination explained, but it was immensely satisfying, and it emphasised how interconnected all the subjects were. In fact, he summed up his verdict in one word: 'Brilliant!' At that point, Watson's was unique in offering the Baccalaureate exams within the Scottish system, and so it was attracting not only internal candidates and candidates from other schools, but pupils from abroad as well.

A splendidly refurbished Centre for Sport at Watson's, with a renovated swimming pool and other state-of-the-art facilities, was opened on 3 October 2012 by the George Watson's F.P and Olympic gold medallist Sir Chris Hoy after various delays because of the general economic situation and recent storm damage to its roof. In the classroom, the

latest technology was introduced too, with iPads being given to teachers for use there the following spring. At the end of the year there were no fewer than 2,374 pupils on the school roll. Gareth Edwards, the Principal, retired in the summer of 2014 and was succeeded by Melvyn Roffe, until then Principal of Wymondham College, Norfolk, England's largest state boarding school.

In 2010 it was decided to rename the Erskine Stewart's Melville Performing Arts Centre. Tom Fleming, the distinguished Scottish actor, had died in April. He had been a former pupil of Daniel Stewart's, and so the building became the Tom Fleming Centre for the Performing Arts. Stewart's Melville had recently been fortunate in obtaining a new piece of property close to Dean Park House. It was a three-storey, open-plan office building put up in about 1990. Its site on the corner of Queensferry Road and Queensferry Terrace had actually belonged to Stewart's at one time, but they had sold it in the nineteenth century, and it stood on the only piece of land in the immediate area not

owned by the school. It was the property of the Nuclear Generation Decommissioning Fund, which had let it to the UK arm of Sopra, a leading firm in IT consulting and services. In 2010, entirely out of the blue, the Decommissioning Fund approached the Erskine Stewart's Melville Governing Council with an offer to sell it to them for £2.25 million plus VAT.

This came at a particularly suitable moment, for Stewart's Melville were urgently planning to redevelop their Upper Junior School. The acquisition of Queensway House meant that the pupils could be accommodated there while their existing building was demolished and redeveloped, rather than having to move into unsightly temporary accommodation put up in the playground. The offer was therefore accepted with alacrity and the purchase was completed on 28 April 2011. Sopra would remain as tenants until the end of their lease in 2012, and the Education Board would receive their rent until then. After that, the open-plan offices would be converted into classrooms and

LEFT.
George Watson's College Centre for Sport (Courtesy of George Watson's College)

RIGHT.
Tom Fleming Centre for the Performing Arts at Erskine Stewart's Melville Schools (Courtesy of Stewart's Melville College)

The Usher Hall (© Rebecca Scott of Steven Parry Donald Photography)

other facilities. Once the Upper Junior School had been rebuilt and the pupils had moved back into it, Queensway House could then either be retained or sold again. Work on the refurbishment of the offices was almost complete by March 2013, at a cost of £750,000, and at the end of that September the pupils of Primary 4 and Primary 5 were duly installed there.

The acquisition of Queensway House had come as a pleasant surprise, and the Education Board had already received two unexpected windfalls a few years earlier. In 2005, when Edinburgh City Council were planning a major extension to the Usher Hall, it had come to their attention that The Merchant Company had certain rights over part of the adjacent pavement. This had originally

entered the Company's possession in 1801 as the result of a generous bequest by George Grindlay, an Edinburgh merchant who had been one of the Company Assistants and who had died nine years earlier. He had left half of his estate of Orchardfield, on either side of Lothian Road, in trust to his only son, but when the son died childless before reaching the age of 25, the bequest passed to George Watson's and Mary Erskine's Hospitals.

In 1848 all the unfeued land on the west side of Lothian Road was sold to the Caledonian Railway Company, but The Merchant Company kept the land on the east side. When the Usher Hall was being built in 1911, the Town Clerk was authorised to spend 10 shillings buying out The Merchant Company Education Board's interest in the adjoining pavement. However, for some reason, Edinburgh Corporation decided not to ask the Company to give them a conveyance for this. No more was heard of the matter until 2006, when the City Council offered the Company £50,000 for the ownership of what may have been that same piece of pavement.

In 2012 The Mary Erskine School had been voted the best independent school in Scotland by *The Sunday Times*, and the following year Stewart's Melville won the coveted title. By then the combined schools had adopted the acronym ESMS, with the description 'A unique family of independent schools for boys and girls'. Despite these successes and the enthusiastic response to the devolution of power to the schools, there was some unease in Hanover Street that the Company might be somehow losing touch with them. The term 'The Merchant Company Schools' had long been a familiar one in Edinburgh, but the general public often seemed not to realise which schools were meant, sometimes believing erroneously that the independent George Heriot's and St George's School for Girls were members of the group. Nor did even some of the parents grasp the fact that the Company actually owned its schools. Alan Hartley, a prominent tax consultant and former pupil of George Watson's, had become Master in 2005, alarming Alistair Beattie, the Secretary and Chamberlain, with his ability to compose his highly successful speeches during the very dinners at which he would be speaking. It was unusual for an Old Master to take up the position of Chairman of the George Watson's Governing Council, but Old Master Hartley later did, in order to strengthen the visible link between the schools and the Company.

The new Education Liaison and Enterprise Committee made a deliberate effort to raise the Company's profile with Edinburgh schools generally. They opened the already well-established Merchant Company Initiative Prize to all the schools in the city, and in 2009 it was won by a pupil from Merchiston Castle independent school who had raised £80,000 for a charity that helped seriously injured rugby players. The second prize went to Boroughmuir state secondary school with an internet project aimed at keeping young people off the streets. Pilrig Park, a local authority school for pupils with considerable learning difficulties, received a Highly Commended certificate. By 2014, the first prize would be a certificate and a cheque for £500. An Apprenticeship Scheme was tried, based on the idea that volunteer pupils would be mentored by Company members, but it proved too difficult to operate and it was abandoned. More popular was the plan for members to offer mock interviews to senior pupils, and the new Merchant Company Charitable Trust was now supporting students suffering financial hardship and encouraging young people to expand their knowledge of business and enterprise.

All this was very satisfactory, and the opening years of the twenty-first century saw further eminent additions to the roll of honorary members. Viscount Younger, the Conservative politician, accepted the invitation in 2002, as did Sir Eric Kinloch Anderson in 2004. Former Headmaster of Eton, he was the brother and grandson of previous Old Masters. Lord Sutherland of Houndwood, former Principal of Edinburgh University, followed him in 2007, as did Lord Cullen of Whitekirk in 2013. A former Lord Justice-General of Scotland, Lord President of the Court of Session and now a life peer, Lord Cullen was famous for chairing the inquiry into the Piper Alpha Disaster and the Tribunal of Inquiry into the 1996 shootings at Dunblane Primary School. The high regard in which The Merchant Company was held

was also evident in the fact that around 20 Masters of English livery companies attended the Charter and Court Dinner in alternate years, while partners who accompanied them were now entertained to dinner in the Royal Scots Club by The Master's Lady.

It was gratifying that the range of members had so much widened since the days when they were all actually merchants involved one way or another in the cloth trade. Now, as well as people like Old Master Douglas Kinloch Anderson who carried on that particular tradition, there were representatives of an ever-widening range of businesses and professions, including Information Technology experts and a funeral director. A new category came into being in 2013 when membership was offered to the Principals of the two schools, in recognition of the fact that their position was actually the equivalent of chief executive officers of large businesses.

It was also notable that in 2013, although there were only 33 female members out of the total 545 Company members, half of those serving on the Master's Court were now women. In 2001 Margaret Allan had become the Company's first female Secretary, and two years later Dawn Burrows was the first woman Senior Assistant. By 2014 Julie Grieve (Regional Chair in Edinburgh for the Prince's Trust – Youth Business Scotland) was Chairman of the Membership Committee; Sandy McCreath (a Mary Erskine former pupil and social worker) chaired the Charities Committee and Katie Ridland (who played a leading role in JCI, the self-development organisation) was Chairman of the Education Liaison and Enterprise Committee. Even more significantly, for the first time a woman was elected Treasurer of the Company. Patricia Denzler spent her early childhood in Northern Ireland, before moving to Edinburgh and entering George Watson's Ladies' College. She then studied for a Teaching Diploma in Domestic Science at Edinburgh College of Domestic Science and went on, with her husband, Samuel, to become a well-

The Crush Hall in the Merchants' Hall (© Steven Parry Donald Photography)

known restaurateur and hotelier, holding the presidency of various organisations including Edinburgh Business-women's Club and Leith Chamber of Commerce, as well as being a trustee of the Royal Yacht Britannia and a board member of Scottish Enterprise.

The actual number of ordinary members stood at 523 in 2014. As the average age was 65, the Company were eager to recruit suitable business and professional people who were established in their careers, but younger. This was not so easy, for social change meant that working couples were very fully occupied and their leisure time was at a premium. However, the Company was making the Merchants' Hall a real centre of activity for members, with business break-fasts, membership dinners (speeches to be light-hearted) and hustings. Early evening seminars were tried, but few attended because parents were usually hurrying home to their families after work. However, exclusive trips to local places of interest were popular and there were thoughts that perhaps a curling club might be formed. The golf club had always been highly successful, and a shooting club was established in 2013.

The Company had also been looking to bring in more income by increasing their letting of the Hall to outside organisations for social and professional events. By 2009 a separate Merchants' Hall Company had been set up to be a VAT-registered company and operate the letting of the hall, the Court Room and the Crush Hall (the reception space outside the Court Room at Merchants' Hall), with Jenny Rutherford as Events Manager. Weddings and conferences were the main source of bookings but, in the difficult economic climate, the numbers had begun to fall in 2011, and so in the spring of 2013 a working group chaired by Deirdre Kinloch Anderson, one of the Company Assistants, was set up to consider what could be done to improve matters. There were mixed feelings in the Company about launching a marketing and public relations campaign, but it was recognised that further

efforts were needed. The Crush Hall had previously been redecorated at a cost of approximately £25,000, and it was subsequently enhanced by yet another generous gift.

As we have seen, in the early twentieth century, Sir Gilbert Archer had a strong connection with the EU Congregational Church in Leith, where he and his wife Alison Gordon Spink were regular worshippers. After she died in 1933 their only son, John Mark Archer, commissioned a fine stained-glass window in her memory. It was designed by Thomas McCrae of Hanover Street and made by the well-known stained-glass artists Margaret Chilton and Marjorie Kemp. It took as its theme Psalm 23, 'The Lord's my Shepherd', which was Mrs Archer's favourite psalm, with allusions to Chapter 5 of the Bible's Epistle to the Galatians, verses 22–3, and symbols of various Christian virtues. Also included were several small panels depicting well-known local landmarks such as the lighthouse on the Bass Rock and the Signal Tower at Leith Harbour. When the church closed and was about to be demolished, the window was subsequently dismantled and in 2012 Old Master Gilbert Baird Archer and his wife, Mrs Irené Archer, presented these small panels to the Merchants' Hall, arranging for the stained-glass artist Christian Shaw to insert them into the Crush Hall windows. Mrs Archer had already in 2001 given a handsome silver nef to George Watson's College, with the names of the Chairmen of the School Governors engraved around its base.

With its long history, tradition had always meant a great deal to The Merchant Company of Edinburgh, and it owns many valuable items which have been given over the years: the silver gilt and other plate, significant portraits and paintings, fine furniture and, of course, the Company

archives. When Brian Adair was Treasurer and then Master, it occurred to him during his visits to the English livery companies that there was no place in the Hanover Street Hall where these important objects could be shown to best effect. There was, however, a dingy storeroom in the basement crammed with old files, books, light fittings and surplus furniture. Access to it was not ideal, but nowhere else was available, and so it was decided in 2005 to transform it into a special Archives and Treasures Room, to be overseen by a new Archives and Treasures Committee, chaired by Old Master Adair. In the evenings, the committee members – Gilbert Baird Archer, Vernon Williamson, John Dixon and Maurice Berrill, helped by the Secretary and Chamberlain Alistair Beattie, his invaluable personal assistant Kathleen Callachan, and the hall keeper Glynn Kay, set to and determinedly cleared out the store, sorting its jumbled contents.

Most of the Company archives were transmitted to the Edinburgh City Archives on indefinite loan, and in 2008 Dr Frances

OPPOSITE.
The two stained glass panels from the E.U. Congregational Church in Leith, presented to The Merchant Company by Old Master and Mrs Gilbert Archer (© Steven Parry Donald Photography)

ABOVE.
Mrs Archer presenting a silver nef to George Watson's College in 2001, watched by Niall Lothian, Chairman of the Board of Governors (left) and Principal Gareth Edwards (right)

OVERLEAF LEFT.
Walter Lothian by Henry Raeburn (The Merchant Company; © John McKenzie Photography)

OVERLEAF RIGHT.
Silver gilt Dutch seventeenth-century nef presented anonymously to the Company in 1958 (The Merchant Company; © John McKenzie Photography)

The Archives and Treasures Room in the Merchants' Hall (© Steven Parry Donald Photography)

Shaw, formerly Head of Government Records at the National Archives of Scotland (subsequently re-named the National Records of Scotland), began cataloguing them for the City Archives on a voluntary basis. Denzil Skinner, a jeweller with Hamilton & Inches for 20 years, photographed all the jewellery and catalogued the books, while Donald Forbes, Senior Paintings Conservator at the National Galleries of Scotland, advised about the paintings and the atmospheric conditions of the room. It was then elegantly redecorated and display cases were acquired, in part from Goodwin's, the Edinburgh jewellers, to show artefacts such as The Mary Erskine School memorabilia, George Watson's account book, James Gillespie's snuffbox, Daniel Stewart's Bible, and school

medals and trophies (including the delightful George Watson's Ladies' College Winkler House Trophy for Good Posture, 1943–64). The ballot box formerly used in the election of new members was also placed there, as well as figures dressed in the schools' uniforms and the uniform of an Assistant. The room was formally opened by Lord Provost George Grubb on 21 October 2009.

Gifts were continuing to flow in, of course, some of them in the form of jewellery. There was the new Senior Old Master's badge, presented by Old Master Gilbert Baird Archer in 2001, and the necklace commissioned in 2007 by Master Chris Masters, the Yorkshire-born former chief executive of Christian Salvesen. This was for Masters' Ladies to wear on formal occasions.

It incorporates a former Masters' Ladies' brooch with the addition of a freshwater pearl and matching drop, suspended from an 18-carat white gold neck chain. In 2010 Nick Ryden donated an Old Master's badge in honour of his father, Kenneth Ryden, to be worn by a royal Old Master when present at a company function or, in a royal Old Master's absence, by the second Senior Old Master.

The Company's collection of sculpture was also enhanced by a new acquisition, though in sad circumstances. As had happened with Master John Macmillan in 1901, Master Kenneth Dunbar regrettably died in office on 11 April 2013. A solicitor and a much-respected member of Edinburgh's legal community, he had worked tirelessly for various charities and he was much loved for his warmth, his even-handed manner and tact when chairing meetings, and his dry sense of humour. Giving the eulogy at his funeral, Alistair Beattie recalled an amusing incident that vividly conveyed his manner. When Master Dunbar was first elected, he had a conversation with Kathleen Callachan, who had joined the Company in 1974 at the age of 16 and would rise to the position of Personal Assistant to the Secretary and Chamberlain. She remarked jokingly to him, 'Master, I hope you won't be changing too much.' 'Quite a lot!' replied Master Dunbar, 'and I tell you what, you'll be the first to go!' The twinkle in his eye actually said, 'You are a valued member of staff and you and I are going to get along just fine' – which, of

LEFT.
The George Watson's Ladies' College Winkler House Trophy for Good Posture, 1943–63 (Courtesy of George Watson's College; © Steven Parry Donald Photography)

RIGHT.
Master's Lady Mrs Ian Watson wearing the official Master's Lady's necklace (© Steven Parry Donald Photography)

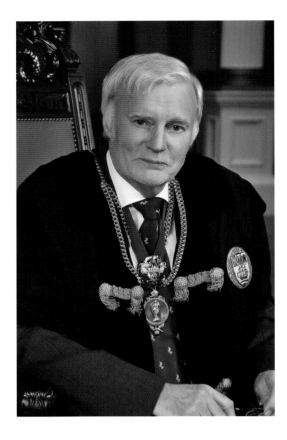

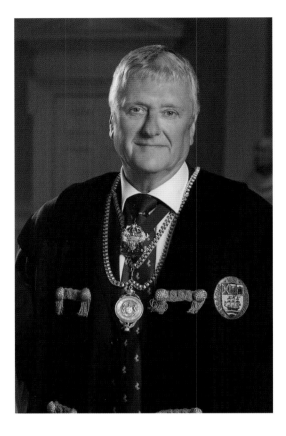

course, they did. In memory of Master Dunbar, the Company commissioned a bronze bust by Laury Dizengremel, the artist-in-residence at Belvoir Castle.

Merchant Company traditions are not only maintained through documents, paintings, jewellery and artefacts, of course. There is the important ceremonial side too. After the death of Master Dunbar, his successor had to be elected within four months of the vacancy occurring, and so on 26 June 2013 Ian Watson became the next Master of The Merchant Company. Educated at George Watson's College and Edinburgh University, he pursued a highly successful career in the seeds business. He then became chairman of Scotland's largest livestock marketing cooperative, Farm Stock (Scotland) Ltd, re-organising it and doubling its turnover. His Kirking as Master took place on

8 November 2013, with the Edinburgh High Constables leading the Lord Dean of Guild and the schools' representatives in procession from the Signet Library across to St Giles', the building with which Edinburgh's merchants had enjoyed such a long connection, reaching back more than 700 years.

They were followed by Bart Dignan, the Company Officer since 1984, in his smart uniform, carrying the Company mace. Behind him came Master Watson, immediately followed by Pat Denzler the Treasurer and Gregor Murray, the Oxford-educated Secretary and Chamberlain whose background is in finance and who is a Deputy Lieutenant of Midlothian. The service was taken by the Reverend Charles Robertson, retired minister of the Canongate Kirk, the Company's Chaplain. There were hymns and prayers, there were readings by Master

Procession going to St Giles' Cathedral for the Kirking of Master Ian Watson, 2013 (© Steven Parry Donald Photography)

Watson and the Principals of the schools, David Gray and Gareth Edwards, and the choir of Erskine Stewart's Melville sang an anthem. The high point of the service was the Invitation to Commitment read by Hamish Robertson, the Head Boy of Erskine Stewart's Melville, assisted by Kirsty Cameron, the Head Girl of George Watson's College and the Old Master and now Lord Dean of Guild, Kennedy Dalton. The new Master in reply promised that he would be true to the office of Master of the Company of Merchants of the City of Edinburgh, and the Master's chain was placed round his neck by the Old Master. The service ended with the Company Prayer and the National Anthem.

No organisation can survive on tradition alone, of course, and the continued lively existence of The Merchant Company of Edinburgh has relied upon its ability to adapt to changing circumstances. Many indeed were the changes in the twentieth century. No longer do horse-drawn trams trundle along Princes Street, past gentlemen in sober suits and top hats and ladies in crinolines. By the early twenty-first century, casually clad tourists in their thousands dodged about among the cars, the buses and the electric trams. Instead of letters delivered both in the morning and the afternoon, emails and texts flew to and fro, and the grandiose meals of Edwardian times had been superseded by exotic cosmopolitan cuisine, takeaways and ready meals. Two world wars altered society in many ways, not least in the position and career possibilities of women, while foreign travel and above all the Internet have dramatically expanded our perceptions of the world. Against this background of sometimes startling transformation, the Merchant

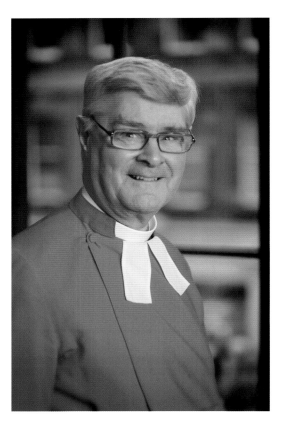

LEFT.
The Reverend Charles Robertson, Chaplain of The Merchant Company (© Steven Parry Donald Photography)

RIGHT.
Old Master Kennedy Dalton, in his Lord Dean of Guild robes (© Steven Parry Donald Photography)

OPPOSITE.
Loving Cup, donated to The Merchant Company by the Assistants, 2003–6 (The Merchant Company; © John McKenzie Photography)

Company has held its own, addressing the inevitable problems with ingenuity, expertise and initiative, the members now saving their schools from being swallowed up by the state system, now augmenting their care for the frail and elderly with purpose-built flats, and generally making their mark on a world very different from that known by their predecessors.

Asked in October 2014 about how he saw the future of the Company, Master Ian Watson replied:

> As we record another 113 years of endeavour and achievement, the Edinburgh Merchant Company continues in good health and is adapting to the challenges of the twenty-first century. I like to think of the Company as a magnificent oak tree grown from an acorn planted in 1681, a potent symbol of the Company's success and longevity. That oak tree has been fed, nourished and cared for by our members for over three centuries, to the benefit of Edinburgh and the surrounding area. With care, attention and good management, going forward that tree will continue to flourish, producing new acorns which, if planted by our members, will have the potential to benefit society still further. I have confidence that our members will continue to strengthen the Company and, above all, continue to safeguard the rich heritage of which we have been temporary custodians.

ABOVE.
Silver rose bowl presented to The Merchant Company by Old Master Kennedy Dalton, Lord Dean of Guild (The Merchant Company; © John McKenzie Photography)

OPPOSITE TOP.
The Master's Court meeting in the Court Room of the Merchants' Hall (© Angela Bonnar of Steven Parry Donald Photography)

OPPOSITE BOTTOM.
The Master Court of The Merchant Company, 2013 (© Steven Parry Donald Photography)

PAGES 198–199.
Portrait of Company members in 2014 by Peter Mennim. (Photographed by the artist)

APPENDIX 1

Masters of the Company since 1681

1681	Sir George Drummond	1715	Claud Johnston
1682	Thomas Douglas	1716	Archibald Macauley
1683	James Nicolson	1717	John Hay
1684	David Spence	1718	John Forrest
1685	Duncan McIntosh	1719	John Osburne
1686	Alexander Brand	1720	Archibald Macauley
1687	Sir Robert Blackwood	1721	Thomas Dundas
1688	John Murray	1722	Hugh Hathorne
1689	William Montgomery	1723	John Osburne
1690	Sir Robert Blackwood	1725	Thomas Dundas
1691	William Menzies	1726	William Hutton
1692	Hugh Blair	1727	William Robertson
1693	Hugh Cuninghame	1728	Robert Blackwood
1694	George Clark	1729	Hugh Hawthorn
1695	Sir James McLurg of Vogrie	1730	John Osburne
1696	Patrick Thomson	1731	Thomas Young
1697	Sir Patrick Johnston	1732	John Cochran
1698	Sir George Warrender, Bart	1733	John Forrest
1699	Adam Brown	1734	Robert Purves
1700	Alexander Baird	1735	Hugh Hawthorn
1701	Hugh Cunningham	1736	Alexander Sharp
1702	John Hay	1737	George Millar
1703	Henry Hawthorn	1738	John Osburne
1704	John Duncan	1739	John Forrest
1705	Francis Brodie	1740	Robert Baillie
1706	Sir George Warrender, Bart	1741	James Stuart
1707	William Baird	1742	Walter Hogg
1708	George Lind	1743	Thomas Fairholm
1709	John Hay	1744	Thomas Young
1710	Henry Hawthorn	1745	Archibald Angus
1711	William Dundas	1746	Hugh Hawthorn
1712	Thomas Dundas	1747	John Forrest
1713	William Robertson	1748	David Inglis
1714	John Osburne	1749	John Dunsmure

1750	Alexander Scott	1801	Alexander Wallace
1751	James Allan	1802	Sir William Forbes, 6th Bart
1752	Archibald Wallace	1803	George Kinnear
1753	Walter Hogg	1804	William Ramsay, Jr
1754	Archibald Angus	1805	Robert Scott Moncrieff
1755	Alexander Scott	1806	Alexander Allan
1756	John Forrest	1807	Archibald McKinlay
1757	Archibald Wallace	1808	Alexander Bonar
1758	Robert Lithgow	1809	James Carfrae
1759	James Stewart	1810	William Creech
1760	John Forrest	1811	Samuel Anderson
1761	William Callender	1812	Andrew Bonar
1762	Alexander Brown	1813	George White
1763	Thomas Hogg	1814	Sir John Hay, Bart.
1764	Alexander Brown	1815	William Ramsay
1765	John Forrest	1816	David Kinnear
1766	Archibald Wallace	1817	William Patison
1767	John Dalrymple	1818	Sir William Forbes, 7th Bart
1768	William Callender	1819	William Trotter
1769	John Forrest	1820	Walter Brown
1770	John Inglis	1821	Robert Hall
1771	William Alexander	1822	John Balfour
1772	Claud Inglis	1823	John Horner
1773	Alexander Brown	1824	Archibald Anderson
1774	John Mossman	1825	Sir James Spittal
1775	John Dalrymple	1826	Alexander Henderson
1776	Alexander Hunter		Sir James Spittal
1777	Alexander Scott	1827	Charles Baxter
1778	Thomas Elder	1828	Alexander Craig
1779	James Stodart	1829	Thomas Allan
1780	Sir James Stirling, Bart	1830	Adam Black
1781	John Fyfe	1831	Robert Scott
1782	David Milne	1832	John Macfie
1783	Alexander Brown	1833	Peter Lamond
1784	Neil McVicar	1834	John Lauder
1785	Thomas Tod	1835	Andrew Miller
1786	Sir William Forbes, 6th Bart	1836	Archibald Thomson
1787	John Gairdner	1837	Robert Thomson
1788	William Ramsay of Barnton	1838	James Hill
1789	Alexander Houston	1839	William Oliphant
1790	Charles Cowan	1840	James Gifford
1791	Robert Young	1841	Alexander Jamieson
1792	Robert Forrester	1842	Thomas Greig
1793	James Mansfield	1843	James Peter Mitchell
1794	Sir James Stirling, Bart	1844	Robert Grieve
1795	Samuel Anderson	1845	James McLaren
1796	Walter Lothian	1846	William Whitehead
1797	George Kinnear	1847	John Stark
1798	Sir William Fettes, Bart	1848	Thomas Sibbald
1799	Sir John Hay, Bart.	1849	James Blackadder
1800	Andrew Bonar	1850	James Gall

1851	James Wilson
1852	Charles Macgibbon
1853	George E. Russell
1854	Robert Walker
	George E. Russell
1855	James Craig
1856	Charles Lawson
1857	James Richardson
1858	Robert Chambers
1859	Charles Cowan
1860	George Lorimer
1861	Charles Lawson
1862	Hugh Rose
1863	James Blackadder
1865	James S. Duncan
1868	Sir Thomas J. Boyd
1871	Thomas Knox
1872	John Clapperton
1874	Robert Bryson
1877	David Dickson
1879	Sir James Falshaw, Bart
1881	Josiah Livingston
1883	Sir Thomas Clark, Bart
1885	Robert Younger
1886	John Gifford
1888	Sir Andrew McDonald
1890	Francis Black
1891	J. Turnbull Smith
1893	John Herdman
1895	W.W. Robertson
1897	Robert Weir
1899	John Macmillan
1901	Robert Weir
	Sir John Cowan DL LLD
1903	John Harrison CBE LLD
1905	William Grant
1907	James L. Ewing LLD
1910	George Lorimer
1911	Sir John M. Clark, Bart
1913	Sir John R Findlay, Bart, KBE DL LLD
1915	W. Fraser Dobie
1917	Alexander Darling LLD
1919	Andrew Henderson
1921	Sir Malcolm Smith KBE
1922	J.W. Shennan
1924	Michael A.T. Thomson
1926	Charles W. Allan
1928	W. Stewart Morton
1930	Sir Gilbert Archer
1932	Andrew Wilson OBE DL
1934	R.H. Munro
1936	William Kinloch Anderson
1938	John G. Galloway
1940	D.W. Pentland
1941	John L. White CBE DL
1943	John S. Blair
1945	William Turner Ewing DSO
1947	William Drummond CBE MC DL
1949	Iver R.S. Salvesen TD
1951	Andrew Dick Wood JP
1953	Stanley Bennet
1955	Robert Wilson MBE TD
1957	James Kennedy OBE DL
1959	J.R. Watherston TD DL
1961	James B. Allan CBE TD DL
1963	William Fergus Harris JP
1965	HRH The Prince Philip, Duke of Edinburgh KG KT
1966	Ian Forbes
1968	W. Grierson Macmillan DL
1970	W.S. McIntosh Reid MC TD
1972	Hugh Rose CBE DSO TD DL
1974	H.P. McMaster TD
1976	Kenneth Ryden MC DL
1978	William T Stevenson CBE DL
1980	R.C.H. Boothman DFC
1982	Adam Currie
1984	Charles D Paterson
1986	Michael J Walker OBE
1988	Sir Peter Heatly CBE DL
1990	Douglas Kinloch Anderson OBE
1992	James Miller CBE
1994	Ewan Brown CBE
1995	Frank Kidd
1997	Gilbert B Archer DL
1999	Ian C Adam
2000	Ian M Darling
2001	John Torrie
2002	HRH The Princess Royal
2003	Brian Adair
2005	Alan J Hartley
2007	Christopher Masters CBE
2009	Kennedy Dalton
2011	Kenneth Dunbar
2013	Ian M.L. Watson

APPENDIX 2

Clerks of the Company
since 1681

(later renamed Secretary, then Secretary and Chamberlain)

1681	Hugh Stevenson, Clerk Depute to HM Scottish Privy Council	1859	Thomas Strong, sole Clerk
1686	Daniel Macpherson	1869	Alexander Kirk Mackie, conjoined with Thomas Strong
1689	Robert Russell	1870	Alexander Kirk Mackie, sole Clerk
1697	Charles Mitchell	1889	Alexander Heron
1725	Robert Rose	1913	A.C. Drummond
1748	Edward Rutherford	1925	George Stuart
1766	James Forrest, conjoined with Edward Rutherford	1936	Catherwood Craig Learmonth
1781	James Forrest, sole Clerk	1946	Harvey M. Harvey-Jamieson OBE TD DL
1783	James Jollie, conjoined with James Forrest	1971	William McDonald JP
1787	James Jollie, sole Clerk	1990	Roger Carus
1825	Walter Jollie, conjoined with James Jollie, his father	1991	Robin Wilson
1846	Walter Jollie, sole Clerk	2001	Margaret Allan
1858	Thomas Strong, conjoined with Walter Jollie	2004	Alistair Beattie
		2008	Nigel Fairhead
		2011	Alistair Beattie
		2012	Gregor Murray DL

APPENDIX 3

Honorary Members of
the Company since 1902

(when the first Honorary Members were admitted)

June 1902	The Rt Hon The Earl of Rosebery KG KT
June 1902	The Rt Hon Lord Balfour of Burleigh KT GCMG GCVO
June 1902	Andrew Carnegie LLD
January 1904	The Rt Hon Lord Strathcona GCMG GCVO
January 1905	The Rt Hon Sir Henry Craik Bt KCB
March 1907	The Rt Hon The Earl of Elgin and Kincardine KG GCSI GCIE
March 1907	The Rt Hon The Earl of Balfour KG
October 1909	The Rt Hon The Earl of Mar and Kellie KT
October 1909	The Rt Hon Lord Pentland GCSI GCIE
October 1909	Sir William Turner KCB
March 1918	The Rt Hon Viscount Finlay GCMG
March 1918	Sir James Alfred Ewing KCB FRS
June 1918	The Rt Hon Andrew Bonar Law
June 1918	The Rt Hon Lord Alness GBE
March 1922	Sir John Struthers KCB
October 1925	The Rt Hon Earl Baldwin KG
March 1929	Sir George Macdonald KCB
October 1931	HRH The Duke of Kent KG KT
October 1931	The Most Hon The Marquis of Linlithgow KT GCSI GCIE
October 1931	The Rt Hon Sir Thomas Barnby Whitson
March 1936	Sir William McKechnie KBE CB
March 1938	The Rt Hon Neville Chamberlain FRS
November 1940	The Rt Hon Sir Winston Churchill KG OM CH
October 1941	The Hon John Gilbert Winant Hon CBE
October 1943	The Rt Hon The Earl of Woolton CH
October 1943	Sir Thomas Henry Holland KCSI KCIE FRS
October 1943	The Rt Hon Viscount Waverley GCB OM GCSI GCIE
October 1943	Field-Marshal The Rt Hon Jan Christiaan Smuts OM CH
March 1949	HRH The Princess Elizabeth, Duchess of Edinburgh (now Her Majesty Queen Elizabeth, Patron of the Company)
March 1949	HRH The Prince Philip, Duke of Edinburgh KG KT OM GBE PC
March 1951	The Rt. Hon Lord Cooper of Culross OBE
March 1951	The Very Rev Charles Laing Warr GCVO DD
March 1951	James Cameron Smail OBE LLD

June 1953	Admiral of the Fleet The Rt Hon Viscount Cunningham of Hyndhope KT GCB OM DSO
June 1953	Sir Edward Appleton GBE KCB FRS
November 1956	The Rt Hon Lord Bilsland of Kinrara KT MC
November 1959	The Rt Hon The Earl of Mar and Kellie KStJ JP
November 1959	The Rt Hon The Earl of Kilmuir GCVO
November 1959	The Rt Hon Viscount Dunrossil MC
May 1962	The Rt Hon The Earl of Rosebery KT DSO MC
October 1962	HM The King of Norway KG KT GCB
October 1967	HM Queen Elizabeth, The Queen Mother
February 1970	The R. Hon Lord Erskine of Rerrick GBE KStJ DL LLD
October 1972	The Rt Hon The Lord Home of the Hirsel KT PC DL
November 1973	The Rt Hon Lord Clydesmuir KT CB MBE TD LLD DSc
November 1973	The Rt Hon The Earl of Elgin and Kincardine KT JP DL
October 1977	The Hon Lord Birsay KT CBE TD DL
July 1979	HRH The Prince of Wales KG KT GCB PC
September 1981	His Grace The Duke of Buccleuch and Queensberry KT JP VRD
September 1985	The Rt Hon The Lord Maclean of Duart and Morvern KT GCVO KBE PC
June 1988	The Rt Hon The Lord Mackay of Clashfern KT PC FRSE
February 1993	The Rt Hon The Lord Macfarlane of Bearsden KT DL FRSE
October 1997	HRH The Princess Royal KG LT GCVO QSO
December 1998	Lady Marian Fraser LT
January 2002	The Rt Hon Viscount Younger of Leckie KT KCVO TD DL
November 2004	Sir Eric Kinloch Anderson KT MA MLitt FRSA
September 2007	Lord Sutherland of Houndwood KT FBA FRSE
September 2013	The Rt Hon The Lord Cullen of Whitekirk KT PC FRSE

APPENDIX 4

Land and Properties under control of The Edinburgh Merchant Company at the turn of the twentieth century

Compiled by Old Master Brian Adair

At the turn of the twentieth century The Merchant Company owned substantial land holdings throughout Scotland, stretching from Kelso in the Borders to Peterhead in Aberdeenshire. These had arisen through both land purchase and bequests to the schools or to the Company itself.

At that time land bought for feuing, where the seller retained the superiority interest, was a popular investment. Feuing enabled the superior to impose an annual feu duty (payment of a sum by the owner to the superior) and to impose certain restrictive conditions. These conditions required an owner wishing to make changes to the use of the land, to seek consent or waiver from the superior which often came at a price, making ownership of superiorities a valuable asset.

As a feudal superior, The Merchant Company received many requests for waivers and profited as a result, and although the market in superiority interests was effectively ended by the Land Tenure Reform (Scotland) Act 1974 – which made the redemption of most feu duties compulsory on sale and prohibited the creation of new ones – the ability to charge for granting consents or waivers continued until 2004, when the feudal system was abolished and superiority interests in land ceased to exist (Abolition of Feudal Tenure etc. (Scotland) Act 2000).

In addition to the properties acquired by The Company between 1728 and 1889 (7,774.5 acres at a total cost of £154,969), by 1891 it had purchased feu duties for the Widows' Fund in Edinburgh at Trinity, Greenbank, Merchiston and Archibald Place,

and for Daniel Stewart's Hospital at Braidburn Crescent, South Bridge, High Street, East Cross Causeway, Charles Street and Niddrie Street. The Governors of the Merchant Maiden Hospital owned what was known then as The Edinburgh Ladies' College in Queen Street, the Governors of George Watson's Boys College owned the school at Archibald Place and the Governors of George Watson's Ladies' College owned property in George Square. Furthermore, the Governors of James Gillespie's Hospital had property at Windmill Street and a house at 22 Merchiston Park, and the William Watherston Endowment owned all the properties between 1 and 13 Drumsheugh Place.

Few of the above properties still remain in Company ownership, with many having been sold to fund the school estates or the Company's charitable trusts under the umbrella of either the Education Board or The Merchant Company Endowments Trust. Also, the end of the feudal system of land tenure meant that Merchant Company feudal superiorities became practically worthless.

Property has served the Company well both in terms of income and capital growth over the centuries. For example, in 1959–60 the rent of the houses and shops at Drumsheugh Place was £2,772. In 2014 the rents from the shops and car parking to the rear (the flats having been sold for over £0.5m in the 1990s) was £184,753 – almost 70 times the income in 1959.

Without doubt, the most valuable asset ever

gifted to the Company was the nursing home at Pitsligo House in 1966, the sale of which in 2003 permitted the Endowments Trust to purchase an office block in Albany Street and to build a total of 68 flats for the frail and elderly at Brandfield Street and Little Road. In 2014 the property assets held within the Endowments Trust had an estimated value of over £16m.

The Company's Estates

DANIEL STEWART'S HOSPITAL

The Estate of Bathgate and Balbardie
Comprising 854 acres. Acquired in 1861 at a cost of £48,000

This estate was situated within the County of Linlithgow and included the whole town. Balbardie Estate consisted of the mansion house, farms, the Glen Mavis Distillery, a quarry, a limestone works, sandpit and a coal mine.

The Property at Dean, Edinburgh
Comprising 11.5 acres. Acquired in 1836 at a cost of £2,000

This land on the south side of Queensferry Road was purchased from Sir John Nisbet for the erection of Daniel Stewart's College. A small number of feus were given up but were reacquired over the years.

MERCHANT MAIDEN'S HOSPITAL

The Peterhead Estate
Extending to 2,674 acres. The greater part was acquired in 1728 at a cost of £3,240, followed by Grange and Blackhouse Farms in 1783 at a cost of £3,886, with the remainder of the estate acquired between 1831 and 1837 at a cost of £1,508. The total cost of the Peterhead Estate was £8,814.

The Peterhead Estate was confiscated from the last Earl Marischal after the rebellion of 1715 and sold to the Fishing Company of Scotland, from whom the Governors of The Merchant Maiden Hospital acquired it in 1728. The remainder of the estate was purchased from the Yorkshire Building Society in 1783. The Governors of The Merchant Maiden Hospital were superiors of the town and harbour of Peterhead.

GEORGE WATSON'S HOSPITAL

The Estate of Cockburn
Comprising 1,017 acres. Acquired in 1729 at a cost of £2,415.

The estate lay in the Parish of Currie in an upland part of the County of Edinburgh, and contained four farms and about 140 acres of plantations.

The Estate of Merchiston
Comprising 340 acres. Acquired in 1729 at a cost of £11,659.

This valuable estate lay immediately to the west and south-west of Edinburgh. In 1838 the Trustees of the Royal Lunatic Asylum feued over 39 acres. A large area on the north side of the estate was feued to Bernard's Brewery and the large villas in Merchiston, East Castle and Abbotsford commanded sites for high feu duties.

The Roxburgh Estate
Comprising a total of 1,584 acres, this estate comprised two excellent farms – Spylaw (697 acres) and Heiton (887 acres). Spylaw, now rated as one of the best farms in the Borders, was acquired for £3,397 and Heiton for £5,236.

The Estate of Preston
Comprising 95 acres. Acquired in 1752 at a cost of £2,535.

This relatively small estate was purchased from James Erskine of Grange and lies in the Parish of Prestonpans. The rights to the coal and fire clay on the land were let.

The Estate of Gilmerton
Comprising 464 acres. Acquired in 1864 at a cost of £18,620

On this estate, located about four miles from St Andrews, there stood a mansion house, offices, a farm, a steading and a water-driven threshing mill.

The Estate of Falconhall
Comprising 18 acres. Acquired in 1889 at a cost of £33,000

This property occupied the slopes of Morningside from Newbattle Terrace to Canaan Lane, and was ideal for feuing.

The Estate of Spylaw and Bonaly

Comprising 693 acres. Acquired in 1799 as an endowment left to the Company by James Gillespie.

This estate lay in the Parish of Colinton, within four miles of the city of Edinburgh. Principal leaseholds on the estate were Bonaly and Fernielaw Farms, the mansion house of Spylaw, the lands at Spylaw Bank, Spylaw Bank House and fields at the Curriemuir end. Due to the close proximity of the estate to Edinburgh by railway, it was especially well adapted for feuing. One of the principal feuars was Dr Rowand Anderson, who erected several fine villas.

The Property of Wright's Houses,
Bruntsfield Links

Comprising 8 acres. Acquired in 1799 at a cost of £2,400

This property was purchased in 1799 for the erection of a hospital for old men and women, and was used at the end of the nineteenth century as James Gillespie's School for Boys and Girls. At one time there was an old mansion house belonging to a branch of the Napier family called Wrychtis-housis or Wryttes-Houses, but it was pulled down by the Governors to make room for the Hospital. The feus on this valuable site were taken up very quickly.

George Grindlay's Trust –
The Estate of Orchardfield

Comprising 12 acres. Half of the estate was acquired in 1801 for the legal costs incurred by the Trustees of £790, with the remaining half acquired from George Grindlay's Trustees in 1858 at a cost of £14,753.

The *pro indiviso* half of this estate, situated in and near Lothian Road, was bequeathed in trust to George Watson's Hospital. In 1848 all the unfeued land to the west of Lothian Road was sold to the Caledonian Railway Company, and in 1858 the *pro indiviso* half share from John Grindlay's trustees was acquired. The feus included Cambridge Street, Castle Terrace, Cornwall Street, Grindlay Street, Bread Street, Morrison Street and Lothian Road.

Index